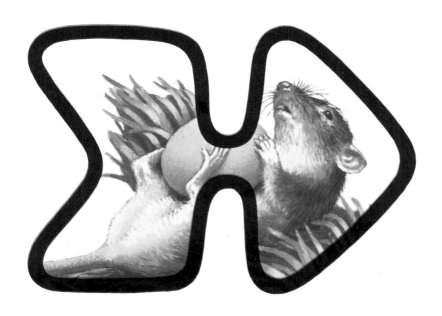

Cassell & Company Limited
35 Red Lion Square, London, WC1R 4SG
and at Sydney, Auckland, Toronto, Johannesburg,
an affiliate of
Macmillan Publishing Co., Inc.,
New York.

Designed and produced for Cassell & Company by
Intercontinental Book Productions
Berkshire House, Queen Street, Maidenhead, Berks.
Copyright © 1976 by Intercontinental Book Productions.

First published 1976
ISBN 0 304 29739 9
Printed in Yugoslavia

The
Biggest Smallest
Fastest Strangest
Book

Written by Cliff Andrew

CASSELL
London

CONTENTS

Acknowledgements
The author and publishers wish to thank the following for supplying transparencies and photographs: Charles Parr (Komodo dragon); Satour (Kimberley Diamond Mine, ostrich on page 14); British Tourist Authority (tapestry); Japan National Tourist Organization (fireworks, Japanese train); Leicestershire Museums and Art Galleries (Daniel Lambert portrait); Ardea Photographics (nephila spider, by Leslie Brown); *Express and Star*, Wolverhampton (padlock); Medical Illustrations Department, Charing Cross Hospital (matchstick carvings); *Aero Modeller* (model aircraft); Australian News and Information Bureau (koala bear); Ernest Ibbetson (orange frog).

Note All the information in this book is, to the best of the author's and publishers' knowledge, correct at the time of going to press.

Where could you watch an ear-pulling contest? Whose income in 1927 was £21,500,000? Could you hold a shark in the palm of your hand? Is it possible to build an office block in less than three days?

The answers to these and many other questions can be found in the action-packed pages that follow, complete with pictures, photographs and diagrams. From records of size and speed to real-life stories of some of the bizarre facts and incidents of past and present, the book is crammed with items embracing natural history, travel, sport, art, geography, industry, architecture, music and a host of other topics which defy classification! So if you want to know where dragons live, or read about the parson who pushed a wheelbarrow across the Sahara desert, or check the world record for prune-eating, this is the book for you.

Biggest

BIGGEST flying birds...civil aircraft...battleships

THE KORI BUSTARD of East and South Africa (*right*), a greedy eater whose favourite sweet is a rich gum from acacia bushes, wins the title of heaviest flying bird. Around 13*kg* is an average weight but specimens of 18*kg* and over have been reported. Members of the bustard family in Western Europe, North Africa, Central Asia and Australia are also heavy, with some recorded weights near that of the Kori. Others in the heavyweight division — average about 13*kg* — include the mute and trumpeter swans, white pelican and rare Manchurian crane.

> *THE BIGGEST BATTLESHIPS ever built were Japanese: the 73,000-tonne* Yamato *and* Musashi. *Both were sunk by American forces during the Second World War.*

THE BIGGEST CIVIL AIRCRAFT in service is a Boeing, the 747 Jumbo Jet (*below*). Its wingspan is nearly 60*m*, length 70½*m* and it can carry over 500 passengers at speeds exceeding 960*km/h*.

THE BIRD with the greatest wingspan is the wandering albatross (*above*). Spans of around 3½*m* have been recorded, and the average is 3*m*. The largest captured specimen had a 3·6*m* wingspan.

THE DRAGON IS ALIVE and well and living on the tiny island of Komodo, east of Bali, Indonesia. Here the dragon is no fairy-tale beast but an officially protected animal living in a nature reserve. It is really an outsize lizard, at 3*m* long the biggest on earth. The shy but fierce fork-tongued 'dragons' (*above*) keep very much to themselves in the densely forested centre of the island. But sometimes local hunters penetrate their habitat and spear one of them for its delicious meat, or a photographer who works fast may lure one briefly out of hiding to devour a dead goat or wild pig. The dragon has been known to eat the equivalent of its own weight in wild pigs in 17 minutes. After such a meal it may then not eat again for three months.

THE BIGGEST CARNIVAL FLOAT ever built was a fantastic dragon called Sun Loon. It appeared in a procession at Bendigo, Victoria, Australia. Sun Loon's 60m-long body was covered with 65,000 glittering mirror scales and its head alone needed six men to support it.

THE WORLD'S HEAVIEST DOG is undoubtedly the St. Bernard. The record-holder, Duke, owned by an American doctor, weighed 133*kg* when he died in 1969, two months short of his fifth birthday. The sturdy St Bernard has a heroic history. It is named after St Bernard de Menthon who founded a hospice high in the Swiss Alps a thousand years ago. The hospice has always been a sanctuary for travellers using the Great St Bernard Pass between Switzerland and Italy, at 2,500*m* one of the highest passes in the Alps.

The dog was probably adopted by the hospice monks late in the seventeenth century because of its uncanny sense of direction and sharp nose for scents, and became renowned for rescuing travellers lost in the snow.

In three centuries the St Bernards of the hospice saved some two and a half thousand people and their exploits became known far and wide. In the early 1800s, one dog, Barry, saved forty lives during his life, and his preserved body can be seen in the museum at Berne, Switzerland.

Today there are road and rail links between Switzerland and Italy that make walking through the Great St Bernard Pass rather unnecessary. The pass itself has had a fine all-weather tunnel since the early 'sixties. But though the rescuing role of the hospice St Bernards has ended, their achievements, now far better known than the saint whose name they perpetuate, will continue to be recounted.

BIGGEST mountains...mouse-haul...amphibian...diamond...hole

AMPHIBIANS are cold-blooded, air-breathing verte-brates capable of living both on land or in water. The biggest amphibian is the Chinese giant salamander (*below*), found in the streams and marshes of certain parts of China. It grows to an average length of $1m$ and a weight of $12kg$.

THE BIGGEST UNCUT DIAMOND is the so-called Star of Sierra Leone found at Kono in 1972. It weighs 969 carats (nearly 200g).

WHAT IS THE world's highest mountain? Including the lower slopes, which happen to be under the sea, the Hawaiian mountain Mauna Kea is $10,203m$ high – comfortably higher than Everest. Topping the list for the highest mountain on land above sea level is Everest, $8,840m$ (*above*). The mountain was named after Sir George Everest, one-time Surveyor-General of India, who died in 1866.

These are the biggest on planet Earth but both are dwarfed by the mountains of Mars, recently revealed by the probing eye of America's space-station *Mariner 9*. The Martian biggest is a volcano over twice as high as Everest and nearly $500km$ across its base.

THE WORLD'S BIGGEST man-made hole (*below*) is the Kimberley diamond mine in South Africa, now a major tourist attraction. It took forty years of digging, between 1871 and 1914, to create the $364m$-deep, $457m$-diameter hole. Altogether, twenty-one million tonnes of earth were dug out, all by pick and shovel. The yield of diamonds from this mountain of earth was just 3 tonnes.

THE LARGEST HAUL OF MICE killed by a single cat is 22,000. The killer was an English tabby called Mickey, who earned his keep as a mouser by disposing of that number over a working life of twenty-three years. Mickey died in 1968 after maintaining an astonishing average of nearly 1,000 mice a year.

BIGGEST flying reptile...bomber

A modern and model version of the pterodactyl as it appeared in the science-fiction film *The Land that Time Forgot.*

THE FOSSIL REMAINS of the largest-known flying reptile, the pterodactyl, were found in a river bed of a national park in Texas, U.S.A. in the early 1970s. The size of the bones showed that the creature had a wingspan of over 15*m*, nearly twice that of the previously known biggest pterodactyl, six times that of the largest living flying creature, the condor, and much larger than the wingspan of a modern fighter plane like the *F4*. The pterodactyl lived around 60 million years ago and had featherless, leathery wings. Palaeontologists — people who study fossils — cannot agree about the ability of the pterodactyl species to fly like a bird. Some say that the estimated body weight of such a huge creature could not be raised off the ground by wing power alone. It is in any case called a winged or flying reptile rather than a bird because it is believed the pterodactyl merely climbed to cliff-tops or other high points and then soared to lower levels like a glider. As nobody can be certain of the creature's body weight, the relevant aerodynamic calculations cannot be made, nor can it be decided whether the monster flapped, flew, glided, or managed a mixture of all three.

THE WORLD'S BIGGEST BOMBER is the Boeing B52, the *Stratofortress* (*below*). It has a wingspan of 56*m*, length of 48*m* and bomb capacity of $26\frac{3}{4}$ tonnes and can travel at over 1,000*km/h*. The B52 is capable of carrying an astonishing bomb load: 84 bombs of 226*kg* each in the fuselage as well as a 10,680*kg* load under the wings. The plane's maximum take-off weight is 221 tonnes.

THE OSTRICH, found in North and South Africa, may not be able to fly but is nevertheless the biggest bird on earth. A height of over $2\frac{1}{2}m$ and weight around $150kg$ have been recorded. Ostriches are fast. Flat out, they can run at over $60km/h$ and they also have a mighty kick: one zoo ostrich bent a $13mm$ iron bar into a right angle with a single kick. They will also swallow almost anything, and are particularly partial to padlocks. In one instance, an ostrich died after swallowing a couple.

Not surprisingly, the ostrich lays the largest egg too. It is around $20cm$ long and $1\frac{1}{2}kg$ in weight, equal to two dozen ordinary hen's eggs.

The largest egg laid by a domestic hen had a double yolk, a double shell and weighed $453g$. It was laid by an American white leghorn in February 1956.

The biggest known dinosaur egg was that of a $9m$-long sauropod that lived on earth about eighty million years ago. The remains of one found in France in 1961 indicated a length of $30cm$ and a $25cm$ diameter.

An ordinary hen's egg (*top left*) compared with the eggs of an ostrich (*left*) and a dinosaur.

THE BIGGEST SPIDER is the South American bird-eating spider (*below*) with a leg span of up to $28cm$ and a body length of $9cm$.

BIGGEST gorilla...crustacean

THE LOWLAND GORILLA of Zaire (formerly the Congo) and Uganda is the largest primate on earth. The average adult male's vital statistics are something like this: height 1·7m, chest 150cm, weight 180kg. These measurements make King Kong's a very tall story indeed, but with an estimated height of 20m or more, King Kong could claim to be the biggest fictional primate.

King Kong, at the top of the Empire State Building, fends off the aircraft of the U.S. Air Force.

THE GIANT SPIDER CRAB (*below*) is the largest crustacean in our oceans. This species of shell-covered invertebrate has survived for 650 million years. The spider crabs inhabit the 300m-deep waters off the east coast of Japan, so they are rarely seen. Captured specimens, however, have had claw spans of up to 4m.

THE LITTLE RED ELF, *a 64-verse story by William Wood, is the title of the world's biggest book. Designed and printed by the author, the book when open is over 2m deep and 3m wide. It is on show at the Red Elf Cave near Dunoon, Scotland.*

THE BIGGEST EXTINCT ANIMAL, the brachiosaurus measured around 22*m* in length and weighed about 80 tonnes. Its head was 12*m* above the ground. A skeleton of this mammoth prehistoric beast, which lived around 150 million years ago in what is now the U.S.A. and East Africa, is in a Berlin museum.

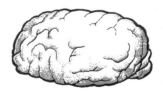

THE BIGGEST MAMMAL BRAIN, irrespective of body size, is the sperm whale's. Its average weight is 7*kg*. The drawing above shows the comparative sizes of a sperm whale brain and a human one.

THE RARE WHALE SHARK, found in the warmer parts of the Atlantic, Pacific and Indian Oceans, is the largest known fish. Specimens weighing 40 tonnes and nearly 20*m* long have been recorded.

BIGGEST eye...octopus...insect...centipede

THE GIANT SQUID has the largest eye of any animal, living or extinct. In the largest species — and squids of 30m overall length have been reported — the diameter of the eye can be as much as 38cm, in other words nearly twice that of a football. The weight of such an eye would be well over a kilo. The largest eye of any *land* animal is that of the ostrich. The average 5cm-diameter eye is, in fact, larger than the bird's brain.

THE BIGGEST OCTOPUS (*above*) is the common Pacific. One caught by an American skindiver in 1973 had a radial spread of over 7m and weighed 53kg.

THE GOLIATH BEETLE of Equatorial Africa (*below*) is the world's biggest insect. This little monstér has been known to reach nearly 15cm in length and 10cm across the back. The South American longhorn beetle is a very close runner-up with an overall length of up to 15cm.

THE BIGGEST CENTIPEDE, despite its name, has only forty-six legs. It is the South American giant scolopender, with a body length of about 25cm.

BIGGEST tapestry...paintings...balloon

THE LARGEST SINGLE PIECE of tapestry ever woven (*left*) hangs in Coventry Cathedral, England. Designed by the painter Graham Sutherland, and woven in Felletin, France, the tapestry measures 22 × 11m and cost £10,500.

TWO CENTURIES AFTER the first hot-air balloon flight there are still enthusiastic balloonists in various countries. There are over a hundred licensed balloons in England, and a small factory in Bristol turns out a couple of hot-air balloons a week for enthusiasts all over the world, especially in America, Germany and Japan. Each balloon costs between £2,000 and £3,000.

A hot-air balloon needs little maintenance and is cheap to run: the fuel bill is around only £3 per hour. But there are snags: before any balloon will take off its envelope must be exactly aligned over the burners to catch the full blast of hot air that will inflate the envelope and lift it off the ground; if there's the slightest wind to prevent this alignment the balloon stays stubbornly earthbound. It's a gentle, pleasant giant once aloft but it's a temperamental one on the ground.

THE LARGEST PAINTING ever produced was American. Unfortunately it no longer exists: it was probably destroyed by fire shortly before the artist's death in 1891. John Banvard completed this epic painting 'Panorama of the Mississippi' in 1846. His subject was a 1900km stretch of the river depicted on a giant roll of canvas 1·5km long and 3½m high.

THE LARGEST SURVIVING PAINTING is probably 'The Battle of Gettysberg' though it isn't the work of one person. It is 125m long, over 21m high and weighs more than 5 tonnes. A French painter, Paul Philippoteaux, and sixteen assistants took two and a half years to finish the work, which was bought by an American in 1964.

THE HIGHEST PRICE ever paid for a painting is £2,310,000, for a Velasquez ('Portrait of Juan de Pareja') sold by Christie's, London, to a New York gallery in 1970. The firm had sold the same painting at auction in 1801 for just under £41.

Below: **at work on 'The Battle of Gettysburg', which is considered to be the biggest surviving painting. A team of seventeen painters took two and a half years to complete it.**

BIGGEST meat-pie...fish and chip shop...income

THE INHABITANTS of Denby Dale, a village in Yorkshire, England, bake mammoth meat-pies to celebrate special royal occasions. Not surprisingly they don't do it very often: only six have been made since the first was baked in 1788. Number four, celebrating Queen Victoria's Jubilee in 1887, went bad and had to be buried. But number seven, to celebrate four royal births in 1964, became the biggest meat-pie ever baked, turning the scales at over five tonnes. The size was $5\frac{1}{2}m$ by nearly $2m$.

Bank robbery was one source of the vast income of Al Capone, celebrated gangster of the 'thirties.

THE HIGHEST INCOME acquired in a year by any individual was £21½ million. The year was 1927, the recipient the notorious Chicago gangster Al Capone (*below*). The whole income was illegally gained by criminal activities of various kinds.

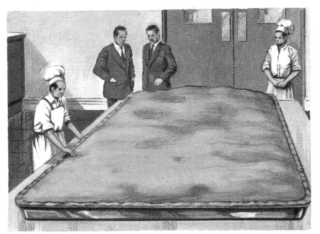

NO LESS THAN 30,000 customers queued to get into Harry Ramsden's, the world's biggest fish-and-chip shop, when they held a special Big Fry night. The famous shop in Yorkshire, England, has claimed the world title ever since it opened nearly fifty years ago. Ramsden's serve only fish and chips — no pies, sausages or chicken — either to take away or to eat on the premises, which means in the restaurant with its impressive chandelier, carpets and stained glass windows.

Some 200 tonnes of fish, 400 tonnes of potatoes, 26,000 loaves and 20,000 bottles of sauce are consumed every year by Ramsden customers, who are served by a staff of nearly sixty people.

BIGGEST firework...crowd...magnet...jigsaw...bicycle

Above: **a Japanese firework display.**

THE BIGGEST FIREWORK is made in Tokyo, Japan. Called Bouquet of Chrysanthemums, it is fired from a 90*cm*-calibre mortar and produces a 610*m*-diameter flower at an altitude of over 900*m*.

THE WORLD'S BIGGEST MAGNET, 60m in diameter and 36,500 tonnes in weight, is in the Institute for Nuclear Research at Dubna, Moscow, U.S.S.R.

THE BIGGEST BICYCLE ever built was a 32-man, 18*m*-long machine made in England in 1974.

205,000 PEOPLE WATCHED URUGUAY beat Brazil 2-1 in the 1950 World Cup at Rio de Janeiro — the largest soccer crowd in history (*below*, the stadium at Rio). That's large as sports crowds go, but small compared with the biggest crowd ever assembled for any purpose: a Hindu festival held at Allalabad, India in 1966 attracted a crowd estimated at five million — twenty-five times greater than the Rio one.

THE LARGEST JIGSAW PUZZLE in area was hand-made in 1975 by a British soldier. It measured nearly 11m × over 9m and contained 1,020 pieces. The largest in number of pieces but not in area has an estimated 40,000 pieces.

BIGGEST trees...leaf...locust swarm

Left: **an impressive example of the Californian Redwood (Wawona) tree.**

THE TALLEST SPECIES of tree is the sequoia or redwood of California, U.S.A. for which heights of up to 112*m* and a girth of 24*m* have been recorded. Other very tall species are the Australian mountain ash or eucalyptus tree, and the North American Douglas fir, capable of reaching 100*m*.

Above: **General Sherman.**

Banyan tree

THE RAFFIA PALM, a native of the Mascarene Islands in the Indian Ocean, and the Amazonian bamboo palm of South America grow leaves up to 20m long, easily the biggest in the plant world.

THE BIGGEST LOCUST SWARM was seen crossing the Red Sea in 1889. It covered an estimated 5,000 *sq km* and was reckoned to contain 250,000 million locusts weighing over half a million tonnes.

The biggest species of tree in terms of area covered by its branches is the banyan or Indian fig tree. The branches that grow from its trunk produce roots of their own which grow until they reach the ground, where they root and develop until they are as big as the main trunk. After a time, therefore, the series of trunks connected to the original makes the banyan resemble a whole wood rather than a single tree. As many as 350 new 'trunks' can grow from the original in this way, as well as several thousand lesser ones. The tree can eventually cover a huge area, large enough for many thousands of people to shelter beneath its branches.

The most massive living thing in existence is generally supposed to be the 2,000-tonne, 83*m*-high General Sherman, a sequoia which has been growing in what is now California for about 3,500 to 4,000 years. It sprung up well before the time of the Egyptian king Tutankhamen and is therefore also one of the oldest living things on earth.

BIGGEST people...planet

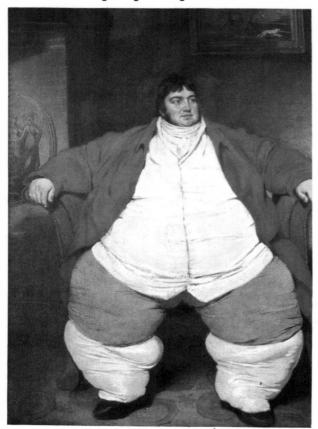

A painting of Daniel Lambert (1770–1809) by Benjamin Marshall (1768–1835).

THERE'S A CERTAIN LACK of evidence and some confusion about the statistics in the human height category. It seems, however, that the tallest giant — and the size is undoubtedly authentic — among men was an American, Robert Wadlow, who was 272cm tall when he died in 1940 aged twenty-two.

There is reliable evidence to suggest that only seven other human males have exceeded 244cm. One of them, American Don Koehler of Chicago, is still alive: he is 248cm high. The other six — two Americans, one Finn, a German, Kenyan and Libyan — all lived in this century.

The tallest woman on record was Jane Bunford of Northfield, England, who was 198cm at the age of thirteen and 231cm when she died in 1922 aged twenty-six. Her skeleton is in Birmingham University's medical school museum.

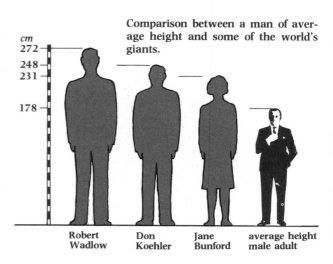

Comparison between a man of average height and some of the world's giants.

cm			
272			
248			
231			
178			
Robert Wadlow	Don Koehler	Jane Bunford	average height male adult

THE HEAVIEST HUMAN of all time was Robert Hughes, an American who died in 1958 aged thirty-two. His greatest weight was 485kg and his waist measurement over 3m. He weighed 5kg at birth and over 90kg as a 6-year-old, much more than the weight of the average adult male.

One of only two Britons to exceed 317kg was the celebrated Daniel Lambert (above), who weighed 335kg. He was perhaps the most interesting, most active and most cheerful of the super-heavyweights. His clothes and other possessions can still be seen at a museum in Leicester. Daniel did not let his weight keep him from riding (his horse Monarch was the biggest in the world, necessarily), walking and swimming. He travelled about the country in a specially built coach and when he died in 1809, aged thirty-nine, the wall of the inn where he was staying had to be knocked down before he could be removed. His coffin was built on wheels and twenty men were needed to lower it into his grave. His tombstone inscription has one unique feature: his vital statistics.

The greatest recorded weight for a woman is 362kg but that was the maximum possible on the scales used. The estimated actual weight of the lady concerned, Pearl Washington of Milwaukee, U.S.A., was nearer 400kg. She died aged forty-six in 1972.

THE BIGGEST NORMAL live baby was born to a Turkish woman in June 1961. It weighed 11kg at birth.

THE LARGEST OF the nine major planets (the bodies in the solar system that orbit the sun) is Jupiter, with an equatorial diameter of 141,920km. Its mass is 318 times, volume 1,313 times that of Earth.

BIGGEST lake...park...desert...country...city

THE LARGEST LAKE or inland sea is the Caspian Sea, which lies between Soviet Russia and Iran. It is 1,225km long and over 370,000km in area.

THE SAHARA is the world's largest desert: it covers an area of nearly $8\frac{1}{2}$ million *sq km*, has an annual rainfall of less than 25*cm* and an average daily temperature of over 45°C.

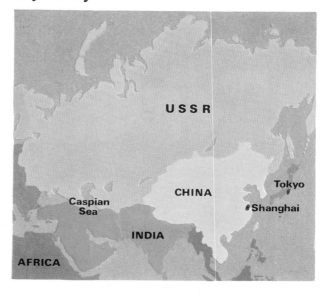

WOOD BUFFALO NATIONAL PARK in Alberta, Canada is the world's largest park, with an area of 45,000sq km.

THE LARGEST COUNTRY is the Union of Soviet Socialist Republics: it is twenty-two million *sq km* in area and covers about 15 per cent of the earth's total land mass.

THE TITLE OF the world's largest city in terms of populations belongs to Shanghai, China: 10,820,000 inhabitants in 1970. In that year, however, the Tokyo/Yokohama metropolitan area in Japan had an estimated 14,034,074 inhabitants. It all depends on what you call a city and how you define its limits. Either way, these two Far Eastern cities are the most densely populated in the world.

Below: **panoramic view of Tokyo.**

BIGGEST disasters

THE WORST DISASTER in the history of flying occurred in March 1974 when a Turkish airline *DC10* on a flight to London crashed soon after taking off from Orly Airport, Paris (*above*). All 346 passengers were killed.

Main Street, Hiroshima, from the Red Cross Hospital building.

THE HIGHEST DEATH TOLL in a single-building fire was 1,670 in 1845, when a theatre in Canton, China was burned down.

THE BLACK DEATH, or Plague, killed an estimated seventy-five million people in four years during the middle of the fourteenth century.

OVER 800,000 PEOPLE died in Shensi Province, China in an earthquake in 1556.

THE HIGHEST NUMBER OF CASUALTIES in a battle was over one million in the First World War. These were French, British and German soldiers killed in the first Battle of the Somme, which lasted from July to November 1916.

THE ATOMIC BOMB dropped on Hiroshima, Japan, which marked the beginning of the end of the Second World War, killed 90,000 people according to American figures, nearly a quarter of a million according to the Japanese.

AN INFLUENZA EPIDEMIC that swept the world in 1918 killed over twenty-one million people in eight months.

Left: troops trudge through a mud-bath that was once a forest – a typical World War One scene in France.

BIGGEST chocolate factory...mammal...ball of string

THE BIGGEST BALL of string belongs to Francis Johnson of Darwin, Minnesota, U.S.A. He has built it up since 1950 and it is now a 3m-diameter ball weighing 4½ tonnes. An anti-theft device is attached to it, oddly enough.

MAMMALS HAVE CERTAIN characteristics which distinguish them from other species in the animal kingdom. A mammal suckles its young, has a backbone, is warm-blooded, well covered with hair or fur and has a well-developed brain.

The biggest living mammal is the blue whale. It is not unusual for the female of the species, which is larger than the male, to reach lengths of over 30m from nose to tail. Although there have been stories of outsize blue whales of 45m, none has been authenticated. The biggest recorded female, caught near the Shetland Islands off the coast of Scotland in 1926, was 33m long. Though the weight was not checked at the time, it was probably near 150 tonnes.

Blue whales can weigh nearly 3 tonnes and measure up to 8½m at birth.

The blue whale's size has also made it a natural prey for commercial whalers. Although it is now a strictly protected species, early in 1963 there were only an estimated 2,000 blue whales in existence, compared with some 150,000 before hunting decimated the stock.

BIGGEST weightlift...teeth-drawn load...cave system

IN 1974 JOHN MASSIS, a Belgian, proved he has the world's strongest set of teeth when he pulled two Long Island railway trucks weighing 80 tonnes along a track with his teeth.

THE GREATEST RECORDED WEIGHT lifted above shoulder level is 240kg in November 1974 by the Russian weightlifter Vassily Alexeyev, latest and greatest of a long sequence of Russians who have dominated weightlifting since the mid-'fifties.

What gives a man the strength to lift the equivalent of a Mini above his head? Body weight and physique are important: Alexeyev has a 121cm waist and 86cm thigh (as big as many a man's chest), and weighs nearly 151kg. Diet is also important: a world-class lifter can get through a dozen eggs for breakfast and a whole leg of lamb for lunch as well as several fair-sized steaks a day. Technique and training play a vital part too, as the improvements in the perform-ances in the world's strongest men clearly show. A century ago the biggest above-the-head weight-lift (known professionally as 'the jerk') was 159kg; only in the last twenty years has the record passed the 180kg mark. A mere two decades have added over 50kg to the record.

But who knows whether outside the long-estab-lished and internationally recognized sport of weight-lifting some even greater weight has been moved — briefly, in special circumstances, and without official recognition? Some years ago, for instance, a slightly-built American housewife lifted the end of a car weighing over 1½ tonnes to release her trapped son. Though she did not, of course, raise the whole car bodily off the ground, who is to say that this untrained amateur weighing 56kg did not establish some sort of world record in that special moment of panic and fear?

Alexeyev's official female counterpart would be the American Katie Sandwina of Boston, who lifted 129kg above head level more than sixty years ago. That long-standing record could remain unchallenged for some time yet. To get some idea of what Katie did, imagine a woman today lifting above her head the world heavyweight champion Muhammad Ali *and* another 28 kilos for good measure.

THE MOST EXTENSIVE SYSTEM of caves in the world is the Flint Ridge system under the Mammoth Cave National Park, Kentucky, U.S.A. It is formed from lime-stone layers several hundred metres thick and covers over 20,000sq km in the states of Kentucky, Indiana and Tennessee. The system's galleries range from less than 1m to nearly 30m high, and are connected by a series of passageways over 200km long. A nineteenth-century French speleologist, Martel, described Mam-moth Cave as 'a monstrous and interminable immensity' after staying down there three days. The entire cave system has not yet been fully explored.

The largest known *single* cave is the Big Room of the Carlsbad Caverns, New Mexico, U.S.A., 1,300m long, 200m wide and 99·99m high.

BIGGEST clock...spider's web...butterfly...plants

THE BIGGEST SUNFLOWER (tallest) has been grown in Devon, England. At 6·4m the top is now up to the roof-level of its owner's house. Coming down to earth, here are some British record sizes for common domestic vegetables and fruit:

Length		Weight	
Tomato plant	6m	Strawberry	205g
Kale	3·5m	Turnip	16kg
Pea pod	25cm	Potato	3kg
Mushroom	1·3m (circum.)	Marrow	27kg
Runner bean	85cm	Cabbage	43kg
Broad bean	59cm	Apple	1·3kg

THE LARGEST CLOCK in the world is in Beauvais Cathedral, France. It is 12*m* high, 6*m* wide, over 2½*m* deep and has 90,000 parts. Designed by Vérité, it was completed in 1868 and took three years to construct.

THE SPINNER OF the largest web is the tropical nephila spider, which can produce a web of 6*m* circumference supported by 'guy ropes' of similar length. The web is remarkably strong and quite capable of trapping small birds or animals. Any spider's web, however, has astonishing strength despite its delicate appearance and many have been known to trap snakes and bats. It has been calculated that a single thread has a strength of about 11,000 kg/cm^2. The nephila can produce a continuous silk filament of up to ¾*km* in length. Though extremely tough and resilient, the thread is virtually weightless.

THE LARGEST BUTTERFLY is the giant birdwing. The female's wingspan can be more than 30*cm*. Lepidopterists (experts on butterflies and moths) consider the birdwings not only the largest but also the most magnificent of the world's butterflies. The variety includes one of the rarest and hence most valuable, for it is found only in the Solomon Islands of the south-west Pacific: one of this kind was sold in 1966 for £750.

Right: the giant birdwing shown in comparison with the more common Monarch butterfly.

BIGGEST hotel...kite...beefburger...ship through Panama

IN TERMS OF THE NUMBER of rooms available, the world's largest hotel is the Rossiya in Moscow, U.S.S.R., which has 3,200. It also has 93 lifts and employs 3,000 people. In terms of area occupied and guest capacity, however, the largest is New York's Waldorf Astoria. It has 47 storeys (as compared with the Rossiya's twelve), and can cater for 10,000 guests, as against the Rossiya's 5,350. Below is the Rossiya Hotel, which overlooks the River Moskva and the Kremlin walls in the heart of Moscow.

A KITE MADE OF OVER 3,000 sheets of paper, weighing over 8½ tonnes, was constructed in Japan before the last war. There is no record that it ever flew.

The greatest recorded height reached by kites is 10,829m, achieved by a series of nineteen linked kites flown by a team of schoolboys from Indiana, U.S.A. in 1969.

IN MARCH 1975 what was claimed to be the world's largest beefburger appeared at a catering exhibition in England. Made by Tiffany Foods of Bexhill-on-Sea, Sussex, the monster meal measured 4½m in circumference and weighed just under 200kg, the equivalent of more than 3,500 normal man-sized burgers. A waste of good meat? No. The beefburger was preserved in a giant deep-freeze and later cut up and eaten.

DURING THE LAST week of its three-month world cruise early in 1975, the 65,863-tonne Cunard liner *QE2* became the biggest ship ever to pass through the Panama Canal. At some of the locks the clearance was only one metre on either side.

The previous biggest ship to pass through was the German liner *Bremen* (51,731 tonnes) nearly forty years earlier.

BIGGEST padlock...snake...car

THE LARGEST PADLOCK, used for securing dock gates, is made by a firm of lockmakers in Willenhall, England. The six-lever giant weighs 45kg.

WOULD YOU CALL the Bugatti 'Royale' (*below*) a beauty? Many car enthusiasts think that it is the most beautiful car ever made, but whatever you may think about its appearance, there's no doubt at all that the Royale, Type 41, was the biggest car ever made for private use. It was almost 7m in length (nearly one third of that was bonnet), weighed 2½ tonnes, and had an 8-cylinder, 12·7-litre engine, and a maximum speed of 192km/h. The chassis alone was said to cost £100,000 in 1927 when the car was first built, at Molsheim, France. Its famous Italian creator, Ettore Bugatti, had set out to create the world's most illustrious car and many would say he succeeded. The engines carried a free maintenance guarantee for the lifetime of the owner. Only six of these so-called 'Golden' Bugattis were ever made, and some still survive.

ALTHOUGH AUTHENTICATED CLAIMS are rare, herpetologists (people who study reptiles) would agree that the largest and longest snake is the South American giant anaconda (*above*). Lengths of up to 36m have been claimed but can certainly be discounted. One 11m specimen was reliably reported, but 6 to 7m is the average length on the evidence of specimens in captivity. Despite its bulk and a 'waistline' that can be around one metre, the anaconda is a swimmer. The estimated weight of one shot in Columbia was around 450kg.

Rivalling the anaconda in length though not in weight is the reticulated python: lengths of 8 to 10m and a weight of 145kg have been recorded.

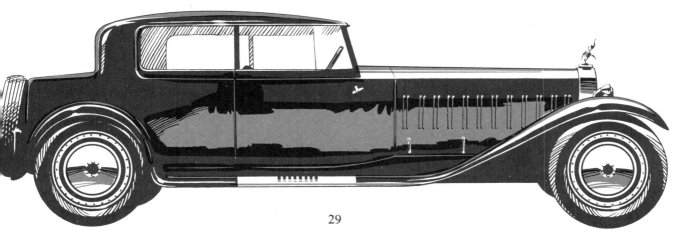

Above: **a 'tube' train draws into a London Underground station.**

Below: **three of the world's tallest buildings:** (*from left to right*) **the Empire State Building, the World Trade Center and the Sears Tower.**

OF THE SIXTY-SEVEN UNDERGROUND transport systems in the world, the biggest and oldest – but not the busiest – is London's, with 405 km of track. However, the 371 km New York subway has more stations: 462 as compared with London's 279. New York's is also the busiest system, carrying 2,000 million passengers a year, more than three times the number who travel on London's Underground.

But London can claim to have pioneered the 'tube' or underground railway system. It was easily the world's first, opening in 1863, nearly sixty years before New York's.

THE 102-STOREY EMPIRE STATE Building in New York enjoyed the distinction of being the world's tallest building from its completion in 1930 until 1970, when the 109-storey World Trade Center in the same city beat it. New York lost out to Chicago when the 110-storey, 443 m-high Sears Tower was completed in 1974. Including the TV masts on its roof, the Tower is 548 m high.

For as long as records have been kept, the tallest inhabited building has been, not surprisingly, in the U.S.A., and for some twenty years until 1974 the world's tallest structure was also located there. But in that year the Warszawa radio mast at Plock in Poland was completed. At nearly two-thirds of a kilometre high – 646 m – it is 18 m higher than the previous record-holder, a TV mast in Dakota, U.S.A. The Plock mast weighs 550 tonnes and took four years to construct.

BIGGEST rabbit...rabbit ears...passenger ships

THE FLEMISH GIANT is the largest breed of domestic rabbit. A toe-to-toe length when fully stretched of nearly 1*m* and a weight of over 5*kg* are common for the Flemish Giant, and one outsize specimen, the heaviest on record, turned the scales at 11*kg*.

Where ears are concerned, the Flemish cannot compete with the lop-eared rabbit (*above*). That's the one with the permanently mournful expression. No wonder — for it has to live with the problem of ears with a span of anything up to 75*cm* and an individual width of 17*cm*.

Rabbits are champion breeders. One domestic type, the Norfolk Star, produces ten litters a year or about one hundred young, nearly twice the average number bred by the wild rabbit. One domestic English rabbit is reported to have produced 40,000 offspring in six years.

FOR OVER A CENTURY, in fact since the first steamship was built, most of the world's biggest passenger ships have been built in Britain. The biggest of them all was the 85,016-tonne *Queen Elizabeth* (*above*), which made its last voyage in 1968 before retiring to become a floating university. The 67,413-tonne *France* (*below*) then became the largest passenger liner in service, and when she was retired in 1975, the *Queen Elizabeth II* (66,917 tonnes) took over the title.

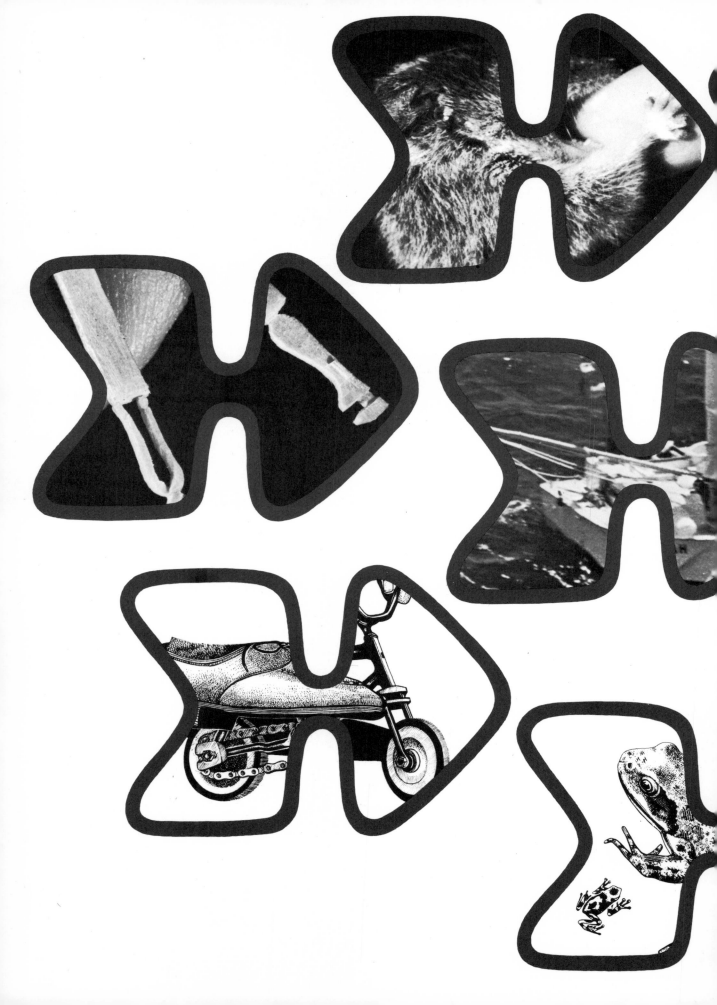

Smallest

THE WORLD'S SMALLEST main-line public railway is the Romney, Hythe and Dymchurch, which runs along a 21*km* 37·5*cm*-gauge track on the Kent coast, England. The locos used are all one-third size models of express engines and include one based on the famous *Flying Scotsman*. A single train can carry 200 passengers at speeds of up to 40*km/h*, equivalent to 128*km/h* for a full-size train. The railway is open all the year round on Sundays, daily from Easter to September.

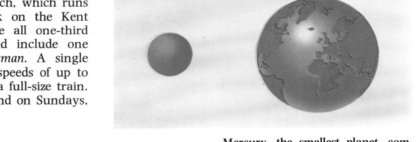

Mercury, the smallest planet, compared with Earth.

MERCURY IS THE SMALLEST of the major planets, with a diameter of only 4,640*km*. As its name suggests, Mercury is the fastest traveller with an average orbital speed of 171,248*km/h*. It is also the hottest of the major planets, its hot side having a maximum surface temperature of over 425°C – hot enough to melt lead.

1	2	3	4	5	6	7	8

THE LESSER MOUSE LEMUR of Madagascar is the smallest known primate. Its length (excluding tail) is between 125 and 150*mm* and weight 45 to 85*g*. The measurement is that of head and body: the lemur's tail is roughly the same length as the rest of it.

CULTIVATING PYGMY TREES, small enough to be grown in a flowerpot, is an art developed by the Japanese. The practice was unknown outside Japan until the turn of the century. The first *bonsai*, as the mini-trees are called, appeared in Europe at a London exhibition in 1909. Though only 30*cm* or so high, the *bonsai* has branches, trunk, bark, leaves, in every way the same as those of a fully-grown tree. *Bonsai* grown from seeds or cuttings will take as

SMALLEST tree...dinosaur brain

long to mature to their pygmy size as their full-sized equivalents in the forest. The mini-tree (*right*) may not reach maturity for fifty years, just the same length of time as the same species full size. Certain trees started in pots are said to be 600 to 800 years old.

THE UNENVIABLE TITLE of smallest-brained dinosaur goes to the stegosaurus (*below*), a 6*m*-long armour-plated reptile that inhabited the earth about 150 million years ago.

Despite its size, this weird-looking monster had a 60*g* brain about the size of a walnut (*see inset diagram*). Virtually brainless, the stegosaurus nevertheless managed to survive in a savage world of terrifying creatures for millions of years. Its long survival undoubtedly depended on its formidable defensive armoury, more effective than that of any other dinosaur. What it lacked in brainpower the stegosaurus made up for in body weaponry. It had enormous bony plates along the whole length of its body to protect it from attack, as well as 1*m*-long spikes at the end of its powerful tail.

35

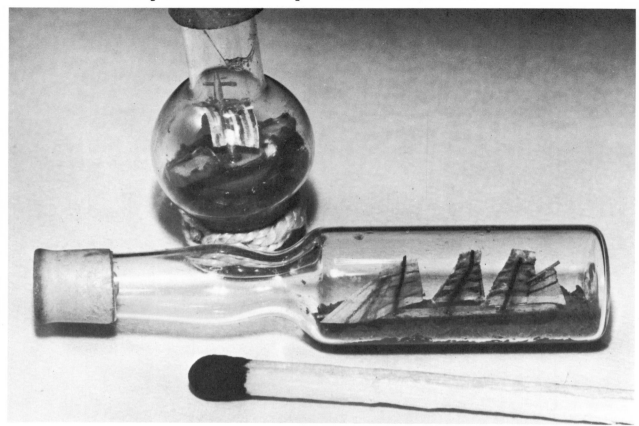

PUTTING SHIPS INSIDE BOTTLES has long been a favourite hobby of mariners. One veteran ship-bottler, Albert Stannard of Leyton, London, is a retired naval man who started over forty years ago by putting ships into large, wide-necked bottles by the traditional method: inserting the whole vessel with hinged sails and masts lying horizontal. Once through the neck and safely installed inside, the sails are hoisted by pulling on the threads attached and then glued in the upright position. Then, adopting a different method, Stannard made the various parts of the vessel separately and inserted them one by one, gluing the whole structure together inside the bottle using a jeweller's watchglass and a collection of specialist tools, some of which he designed and made himself.

After several years he began choosing smaller and smaller bottles to make the task harder and harder. He succeeded in bottling a three-masted ship in the smallest commercially-made liquor bottle (*above*), only 4½cm long, normally sold in novelty matchbox-size cartons and containing a minute quantity of Scotch whisky. Subsequently he found something even smaller to work on: he chose a computer bulb only 12mm long and 3mm in diameter.

Finally he tackled his most formidable task: the 'bottle' is known as a grain-of-wheat, a tiny bulb used in model railways for signals, loco lamps and so on. Even this has been shortened as the threaded end of the bulb has been reduced and re-sealed with solder. The overall size of this bulb is 7mm but the glass length containing the ship is only 3mm, the size of a match head (*left*).

THE SMALLEST KNOWN STARFISH is the Mediterranean marginaster *with a maximum diameter of 20*mm.

SMALLEST marsupial...amphibian...shark

NEAR ADELAIDE, South Australia's capital, in September 1973, Dr Peter Baverstock of the Institute of Medical and Veterinary Science discovered a brand new animal hitherto unknown: a new marsupial mouse. Though the species was known, this particular member of it, accidentally caught in a trap set for lizards in a nature reserve 160km from Adelaide, was not.

The best-known of the marsupials (animals which suckle their young in pouches) is the kangaroo, often as big as a man, very strong and capable of jumps of 12m and speeds of 50km/h. The marsupial newcomer, however, is only 10cm long from nose to tail-tip. Instead of the characteristic blunt nose and large teeth of the rodent, this mouse (*right*) has small, sharp teeth, a pointed nose and, of course, a pouch — which classifies it very definitely as a marsupial rather than a rodent.

Though there are some forty known — and some rare — species of marsupial mouse in Australia, the one that Dr Baverstock found was not one of them, so as well as being among the smallest, this creature is the newest marsupial on earth.

Since the first, a male, gave himself up, a second male has been caught. Then, in October 1974 the Institute captured a female with no less than six young — each about half the size of your little fingernail — in her pouch. The mystery mouse, after close study by experts at the Institute, will be officially christened and classified for scientists throughout the world.

Above: **the Cuban arrow poison frog (*top right of picture*) compared with the most common variety.**

THE SMALLEST AMPHIBIAN is the Cuban arrow poison frog, whose average length is only 10mm. The female arrow poison frog is so small it can only lay one egg a year, compared with the hundreds and even thousands produced by the female of larger breeds of frog. (There is in fact one specimen which can lay as many as 35,000 eggs a year!)

A HITHERTO UNKNOWN TYPE of shark was discovered in June 1908 when a jet-black, white-finned, cigar-shaped specimen was found in a fishing net after a trawl at 170 fathoms in Batanga Bay, Philippines.

Far from being a huge, fierce creature with cavernous jaws and a wicked set of teeth, this new member of the shark family was just 15cm long. Though small enough to be comfortably — and safely — held in the palm of the hand, it was fully mature and could therefore be called the smallest known full-grown shark in the world's oceans.

Marine zoologists officially christened the newcomer with the Latin name *squaliolus laticaudus*. A year or so later an even smaller specimen, a female measuring 11½cm, was captured in the same bay. Remarkably, nothing more was heard of the *squaliolus* for half a century. Then in June 1961 shrimp fishermen in Suraga Bay, Honshu, off the central coast of Japan, caught no less than five specimens each about 11cm long. The Japanese zoologists gave it a name that roughly translated means 'long-faced dwarf shark'.

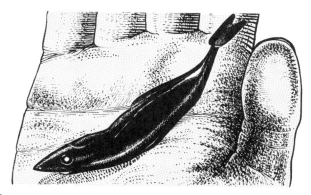

SMALLEST dogs...insects

IN THE INSECT CATEGORY, which covers twenty-nine divisions and about one million known species, the smallest are the hairy-winged beetle and the fairy fly (in fact a wasp, despite its name). These insects are 0·2*mm* long and have a 1*mm* wingspan.

Fairy fly (150 times life size)

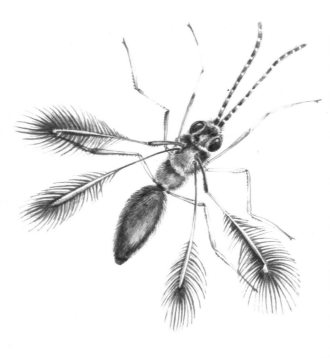

Hairy-winged beetle (325 times life size)

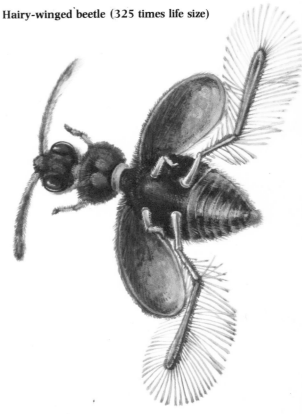

THE SMALLEST OF THE DOMESTIC DOGS (*above*) is the pocket-sized chihuahua (pronounced chee-wa-wa), a native of Mexico. Fully grown, even the weightiest of the breed barely turns the scales at 1½*kg* and the world's smallest, owned by an American, is only 283*g*. There are smooth and long-haired types and the breed is very popular in the U.S.A. where it ranks fifth in the dog popularity ratings. The chihuahua is reputed to have been bred by the Indians for ceremonial purposes, in some cases as a delicacy for their feasts. The Aztecs buried these dogs with their owners, in the belief that this would ensure them eternal life.

Another tiny dog is the Yorkshire terrier, generally regarded as the smallest British breed: one fully-grown dog weighed only 566*g*. The tiniest toy poodle weighed even less, 360*g*, and stood all of 11*cm* high at the shoulder.

Small dogs tend to outlive big ones. The average life span of the Yorkshire terrier is fifteen years, half as long again as that of the St Bernard. But the world record for the longest-living dog of any breed is held by a black labrador called Adjutant, from Lincolnshire, England, who died in 1963 aged 27¼ years.

SMALLEST butterfly...crab...rodent...bird

THE SMALLEST BUTTERFLY in the world is the dwarf blue from South Africa with a wingspan of only 14mm. But the smallest of all the lepidoptera — the butterfly and moth division of the insect world, covering no less than 140,000 known species — is a moth with a wingspan of only 2mm and body length also of 2mm, that is, not much more than the thickness of a matchstick.

THE SMALLEST CRAB is the aptly-named pea crab, so-called because it is just about the size of a pea.

THE SMALLEST RODENT is the Old World harvest mouse. The British version of this little creature weighs up to 9g and measures 11cm at most from its nose to the tip of its long tail.

THE BEE HUMMING BIRD of Cuba is 55mm long and weighs about 2g, less than some moths, which earns it the title of the world's smallest bird. The average wingspan is 28mm. Making up in courage and ferocity what it lacks in size, the 'fairy hummer' uses its needle-sharp beak as a weapon against other much bigger birds, including the eagle. Capable of flying straight up or down, sideways and even backwards, this little bird is a formidable adversary.

THE SMALLEST BOAT to have accomplished the Atlantic crossing successfully is the *2m*-long *April Fool*. The crew consisted of a lone American, Hugo Vihlen, who did the journey from Casablanca, Morocco, to Fort Lauderdale, Florida, U.S.A. in 85 days in 1968.

The smallest boat to cross the Atlantic from west to east (Fort Lauderdale, Florida to Tralee, S. Ireland) is the *3·65m Nonoalca*. American William Verity did the crossing in sixty-eight days in 1966.

THE STATE OF BOLIVAR, Colombia, issued the smallest postage stamps ever from 1863 to 1866 (*below*). The values were 10 cents and 1 peso, and the stamps measured $8 \times 9\frac{1}{2}mm$.

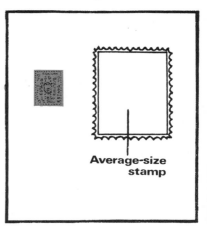

Average-size stamp

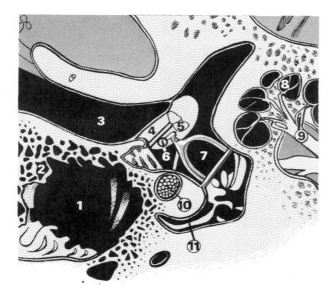

1. Mastoid cells 2. Mastoid 3. External auditory canal 4. Tympanic membrane 5. Malleus 6. Incus 7. Stapes 8. Scala vestibuli 9. Spiral ganglion 10. Facial nerve and canal 11. Lateral semicircular canal

A NINETEENTH-CENTURY fisherman's cottage at Conway, North Wales, is the smallest habitable house in Britain. It is 182cm wide, 315cm high and consists of two tiny rooms and a staircase.

LARRY YATES OF OREGON, U.S.A. produced the smallest writing when he successfully engraved the Lord's Prayer inside an area of one square millimetre. It was done manually with the aid of a pivot-arm device he invented.

THE SMALLEST OF the 639 muscles in the human body is the stapedus. It controls the smallest bone, the stapes or stirrup bone in the middle ear, and is just over a millimetre long. The stapes is longer, about *3mm* on average, and weighs between 2 and *4mg*.

SMALLEST underpass...book...bicycle...tube...church...seed

WHAT IS ALMOST CERTAINLY the smallest underpass in the world has been built under the M5 motorway in England. The tunnel is just 30cm wide and the pedestrians using it are badgers. This safety measure enables these shy animals to cross the motorway without having to risk almost certain slaughter.

THE SMALLEST SEED in the plant world comes from a species of orchid. Thirty-five million of these seeds would weigh just over 28g.

THE SMALLEST RIDABLE BICYCLE is only 12cm high with 5 and 10cm-diameter wheels. The maker and rider is an American sailor from Maryland, U.S.A.

THE SMALLEST CHURCH in the world is in Wiscasset, Maine, U.S.A. It is just over 2m long and under 1½m wide.

THE BRITISH TUBE MANUFACTURERS Accles & Pollock have had a friendly rivalry for nearly half a century with their American competitors, the Superior Tube Company of Pennsylvania, over producing the smallest-diameter tube.

The challenge began in 1928 when Superior sent Accles & Pollock an extremely small tube and challenged them to beat it. By way of a reply the British firm returned the Superior specimen with a length of their own tube *inside* it. The diameter of the 1928 Accles tube was ½mm.

In 1963 Superior produced a ·015mm (outside diameter) tube. Accles replied with what is regarded as the world's smallest tube, in pure nickel with a bore (inside diameter) of ·0033mm and outside diameter of ·013mm (one fifth the diameter of the average human hair). A 12mm central-heating pipe is 1,000 times bigger. A continuous piece of tubing stretching 150km would weigh only 250g. A bundle of 1¼ million of these tubes could be encircled by the average wedding ring.

Although the length of the tube manufactured was only about 20cm, it was put to practical use – for the artificial insemination of bees.

Photo shows smallest tubing magnified 1,125 times.

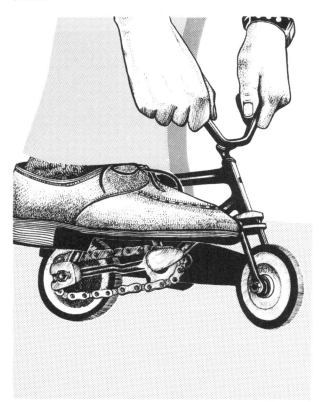

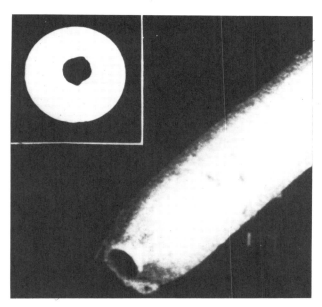

THE SMALLEST BOOK ever printed mechanically with metal type was 3½mm square. It contained the Lord's Prayer in seven languages and was printed in Germany for the Gutenberg Museum at Mainz.

SMALLEST city...country

Above: **the Madurodam in Holland.**

Below: **street-map of the Vatican area in Rome.**

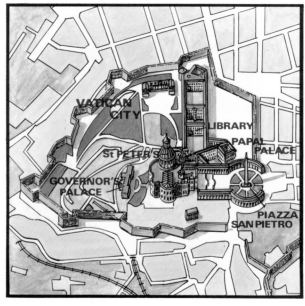

THE MADURODAM at The Hague in Holland can fairly be described as the smallest city in the world. It is a working miniature of a city built precisely to a 1:25 scale, with moving trains, ships, aircraft and people. There are churches, castles, schools, houses, factories, theatres, canals, seaport, airport, stations — in fact everything you would find in a city, working and to scale. Even the tiny barrel organ and brass band play. The tallest building in this city is under a metre high.

The city, named after the founders, Mr and Mrs J. Maduro, took two years to build, was opened in 1952 and has been visited by some twenty million people.

THE STATE OF VATICAN CITY, within the city of Rome, is the world's smallest independent country, covering an area of only 44 hectares or, roughly, that of about 60 football pitches. Its population in 1966 was 880 and its most famous resident is the Pope.

SMALLEST paintings

THE ELIZABETHAN PERIOD (during the second half of the sixteenth century) is not noted for its wealth of artistic talent. Most of the paintings produced were portraits of the nobility, who were concerned only that the result should be a flattering likeness: paintings served to show the sitter's importance and status. Several painters achieved fame as miniature portraitists. One of the best was Nicholas Hilliard, who put life and character into his remarkably vivid miniature portraits of well-known people, including Sir Walter Raleigh (*below*) and Sir Francis Drake (*right*). Many of the paintings, intended to be set in cameos and worn as necklaces, were only about 25 *mm* in size but superbly lifelike and easily recognizable portraits of the subjects.

An Elizabethan miniaturist at work. The inset diagram shows the actual size of the miniatures, while those of Raleigh and Drake (*above*) have been enlarged to show the precision and attention to detail for which the miniaturists were renowned.

ACTUAL SIZE

SMALLEST people

Tom Thumb with his wife (Lavinia Warren) and their child in 1864, when the child was about a year old.

ONE OF THE SMALLEST MEN in the world and perhaps the most famous midget in history, Charlie Sherwood Stratton, was better known as General Tom Thumb, star of American showman P. T. Barnum's strange world of human oddities. Tom Thumb made millions of dollars for Barnum and in the process made himself a fortune too. He sang and danced in Barnum shows before some twenty million people around the world. Only 89*cm* high at the age of thirty, when he died at fifty-one in 1883 he had grown to 102*cm*.

But Tom was not the smallest man in history. Two male dwarfs, one born in Massachusetts, U.S.A., in 1791, the other in New Zealand in 1864, reached the ages of twenty-one and thirty-six and maximum heights of 67 and 70*cm* respectively. The smallest *living* man, an Indian dwarf born in 1929, measures 71*cm*.

The smallest adult human being was a Dutch woman, Pauline Musters, who died aged nineteen in New York in 1895. She was 59*cm* tall and weighed 4*kg*.

How do these statistics compare with those of the surviving pygmy tribes? The African Mbuti are reputed to be the smallest pygmies with an average height of around 130*cm*. However, a tribe discovered recently in Brazil/Peru border country is reported to be on average only 100*cm* high.

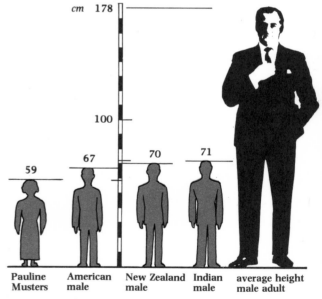

Comparison between a man of average height and some of the world's smallest people.

THE SMALLEST SURVIVING BABY weighed only 283g at birth. She was Marion Chapman, born in South Shields, England, in June 1938. She had to be fed by the doctor every hour with a fountain-pen filler. Marion weighed 48kg when she was twenty-one.

SMALLEST watch...carvings...banknote

THE FAMOUS SWISS FIRM Jaeger le Coultre makes the world's smallest watch. It weighs 7g, has a 15-jewel movement 14mm long, 4·8mm wide and 3·4 mm high. The price range, depending on the choice of bracelet, is from £1,500 to £12,000.

MR RAY COOK OF PINNER, near London, has an unusual hobby: matchstick-carving. He works not by sticking several together but with single matchsticks, each the raw material for an intricate individual carving. His subjects, delicately shaped from the match end, include animals, plants, human figures and everyday objects such as forks and scissors. One fine example depicts a man climbing a palm tree, the leaves of the tree each separately created from the wood, and Mr Cook found the technique of getting the leaves to spread without breaking a very tricky one to master. One of his most remarkable achievements − like all the other carvings, made from a single matchstick without any additional material affixed − is an eighteen-link chain, every link carved individually; the chain

A BANKNOTE ISSUED in Rumania in 1917 measured only 27½ × 38mm and is considered the smallest ever issued.

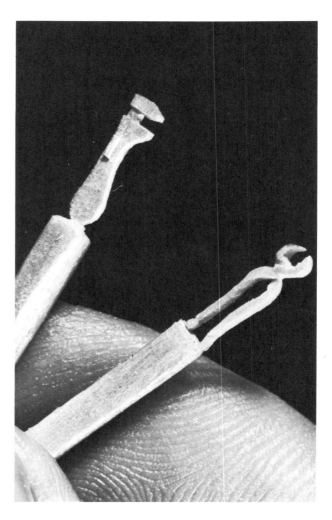

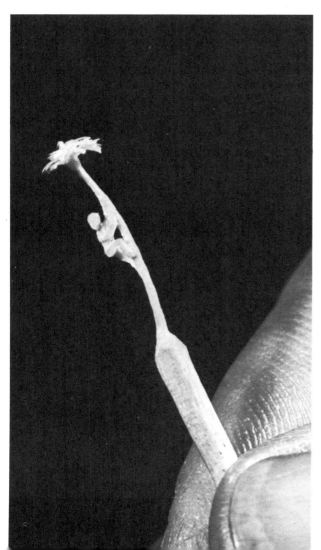

took him eighteen hours to complete. One of Mr Cook's main problems is finding good, sound matches to work on, for the quality of matches varies a good deal and only about ten per cent of the matches in the average box are good enough for this purpose.

Ray Cook has suffered for twelve years from rheumatoid arthritis which has badly restricted the use of his hands. Such a handicap makes his achievement all the more remarkable, for his minute, intricate carvings are just 2mm wide and from 10 to 45mm long (the latter measurement being the average length of a match). His only tool is a piece of broken razor blade with sticky tape wound around one end as a handle.

SMALLEST mammal...horse...spider...fish...ruminant

Right: pygmy shrew, the world's smallest mammal. Some are smaller than a matchstick.

THE EARLIEST MAMMAL was a type of shrew known to exist nearly 200 million years ago, and it so happens that the smallest living mammal today is also a shrew. Aptly called the pygmy shrew, it is only 25/50mm long, weighing a couple of grams at the most. It inhabits the Northern Mediterranean countries and South Africa. Being so small, the pygmy shrew uses tunnels made by earthworms to save itself the trouble of burrowing its own.

Though the pygmy shrew is the world's smallest mammal, there are other species of shrew in North America, Finland and Russia which are only slightly larger.

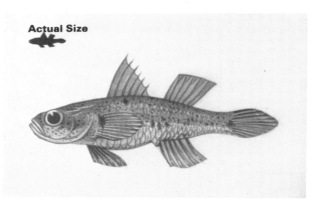

Actual Size

THE ARGENTINIAN FALABELLA is the world's smallest horse. Adults are 38 to 76cm at the shoulder and weigh from 18 to 45kg.

THE SMALLEST KNOWN FISH — and shortest of all vertebrates — is the dwarf pygmy goby from the Philippines. They're so small that a microscope rather than a magnifying glass is needed to study them. The adult male goby's average length is 8mm and weight 5mg.

RUMINANTS ARE THE GROUP of plant-eating and cud-chewing animals: sheep, cattle, goat, giraffe, camel and antelope. The cud is swallowed food which the animal stores in a stomach (or rumen), returns to the mouth for chewing and then passes back into the digestive system. The smallest ruminant is the aptly-named mouse deer of South-East Asia. Fully grown its height at the shoulder is at most 25cm, its average weight 3kg.

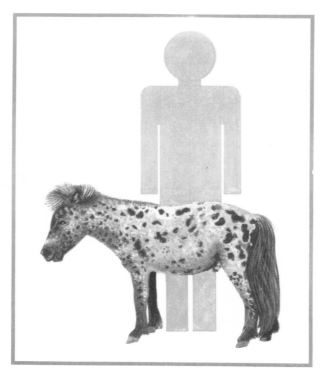

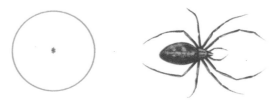

THE SMALLEST SPIDERS are to be found in Samoa (the *patu marplesi* is ·43mm long) and Australia (the *microlinypheus bryophilus* is fractionally larger at ·5mm). The latter is shown actual size on the left, greatly magnified on the right.

SMALLEST aircraft...living thing...cause of destruction...coin

THE SMALLEST PILOTED AIRCRAFT was the Stits *Skybaby*, designed, built and flown by Ray Stits in California in 1952. The *Skybaby* was only 3*m* long with a wingspan of 2*m*, but it was still capable of a top speed of 300*km/h*.

That was over twenty years ago and there's no record of any smaller flying machine having become airborne since the *Skybaby*. However, in 1973 a French aerodynamics engineer, Michel Colomban, built a midget twin-engine, single-seat plane he claims is the world's smallest piloted flying machine. The Colomban aircraft (*above*) weighs only 63*kg* – about the weight of a small man – cruises at 160*km/h* and has a range of 384*km*. It cost only £500 to make and is remarkably economical to run: it will cover 100*km* on only 4·5*l* of petrol, making the plane as cheap to run as a small car.

It is also very portable. In five minutes the whole plane can be dismantled ready for stowing in a car trailer.

Michel's baby has a wingspan of $4\frac{1}{2}m$, double that of the *Skybaby*. The smallest aircraft flying today? If the *Skybaby* is no longer airborne, Michel could well be right.

THE SMALLEST LIVING THING is one of a group of organisms called mycoplasma. During the early part of its life the organism's diameter is 100 millimicrons. (A micron is one thousandth of a millimeter; a millimicron is one thousandth of a micron.)

CHALLENGED TO FIND the smallest living creature that has done the greatest harm to mankind, one could hardly do worse than award that sinister distinction to the rat flea. As the carrier of the deadly bubonic plague bacterium, this lethal bloodsucker can be held responsible for the deaths of 25 million people in Europe during the Middle Ages and over 10 million in India during the great plague period at the turn of this century.

THE SMALLEST COIN was issued in Nepal around 1740. Made of silver, the jawa measured about 2mm and weighed at most ·014g.

London in 1665 when the Great Plague was killing thousands week by week. Caused by bacteria carried by the rat flea, the illness was severe, prolonged and mostly fatal. Infected houses had the sign of the cross painted on their doors, and the dead were collected by the cartload.

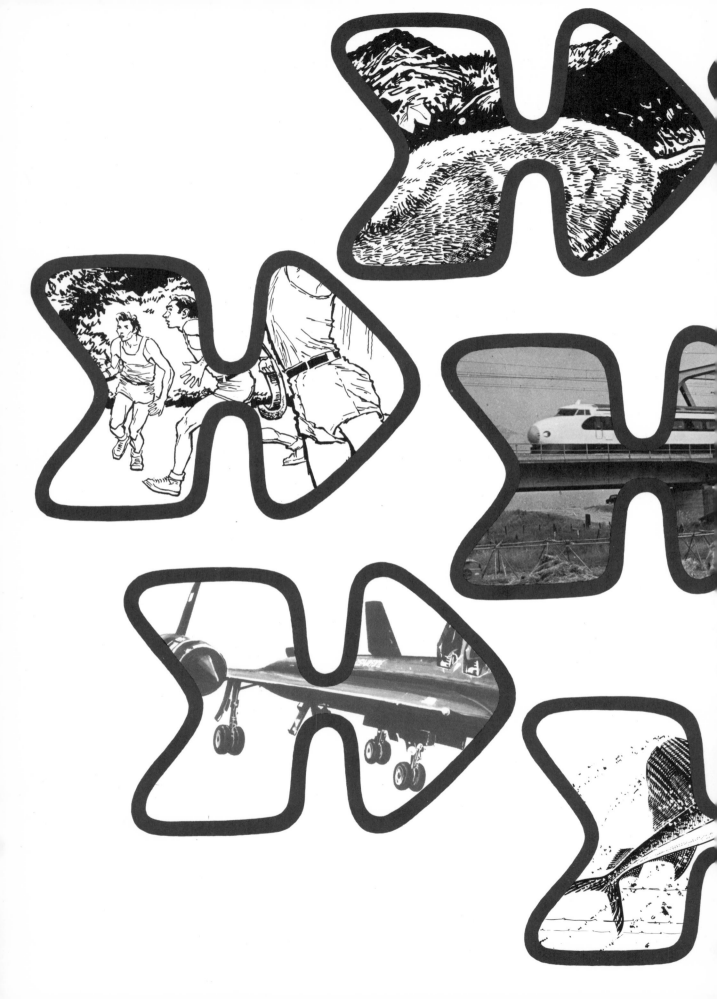

Fastest

FASTEST-growing tree ...tree-climber... animals

THE FASTEST LAND ANIMAL is accustomed to roaming the flat plains and savannahs of Iran, Afghanistan, India and East Africa — terrain which is ideal for speed. Maybe the cheetah (*left*), the proud owner of the land speed title, developed its astonishing ability to run faster than any other animal because of its instinct for survival — by catching its prey and escaping its enemies in the open, exposed places it inhabits.

Certainly this beautiful, graceful member of the big-cat family, taking strides of more than 6*m*, can keep pace with a fast-moving vehicle. Its limbs are longer than those of the leopard, the lion and the tiger, and over short distances it has reached speeds of up to 90*km/h*. However, the cheetah can sustain that speed for a few hundred metres only. It is the sprinter, not the marathon runner, of the animal world.

Over long distances, the fastest animal is a species of antelope called pronghorn (*centre*). A native of the western states of America, the pronghorn antelope can maintain a steady 56*km/h* for 6*km* or more. Indeed, it has managed 88*km/h* — only slightly less than the cheetah's top speed — for nearly a kilometre, and one champion runner reached 104*km/h* over an unrecorded distance.

Therefore, in any animal Olympics, the cheetah would undoubtedly win the 100 Metres, but the 5,000 Metres, where stamina counts most, would plainly be a certainty for the pronghorn antelope.

FOR THE TITLE OF FASTEST domestic animal, it's a close and not very clear-cut race between a special kind of greyhound called the Arabian gazelle or Persian greyhound, more commonly known as the saluki (*far right*), and the common greyhound of the race track. Both have the characteristic deep arch under the body and long, powerful legs designed for speed. Claims of over 60*km/h* have been made for both breeds but the trained professional greyhound almost certainly has the edge for the short distance — say, 300*m*. There's no doubt, however, that over 1,000*m* the saluki would win handsomely.

The saluki, the oldest breed of dog, having first become domesticated about 5,000 years ago, should not be confused with the Afghan hound, a different breed and nothing like as fast (top speed 48*km/h*).

THE FASTEST-GROWING TREE is a species of eucalyptus which has been known to grow 10m in little more than a year in New Guinea. Another eucalyptus tree in Rhodesia actually grew to 30m in only seven years.

AT A PUBLIC SHOW in Queensland, Australia, in 1968, a Canadian called Kelly Stanley climbed up a 27*m*-high pine tree in 36 seconds (*left*).

LAND ANIMALS' SPEED CHART

	km/h
Cheetah	100
Pronghorn antelope	97
Red deer	67
Coyote	56
Cape buffalo	56
Giraffe	51
Black bear	48
African elephant	38
Arabian camel	32
Three-toed sloth	1·6

HOW MANY EYE BLINKS can you make in one second? One or two, four — six, perhaps?

In that time the South American humming bird can manage no less than 90 wing beats and the diminutive midge an unbelievable 1,046. Little wonder that these are the champion wing-beaters of the world.

THE FASTEST RATE OF CLIMB by a piloted aircraft was achieved early in 1975 by the American heavy fighter, the F-15 Eagle. It reached a height of 29,400m in just over three minutes, a climbing rate of nearly 10km a minute, or around 570km/h.

THE FASTEST-GROWING BAMBOO grows at the rate of almost a metre a day and can reach 30m in under three months.

In a three-lap race (each oval here represents a 300m lap), the saluki (red) would probably overtake the ordinary greyhound (white) on the second lap.

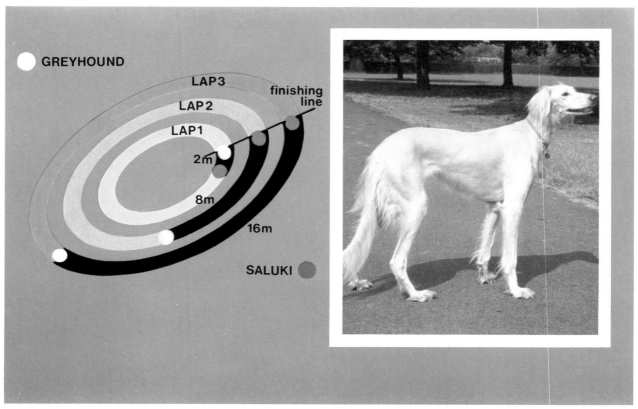

GREYHOUND

LAP 3
LAP 2
LAP 1

finishing line

2m
8m
16m

SALUKI

FASTEST runners

THE WORLD'S FASTEST RUNNERS are the six Americans who have covered the 100m track in 9·9 seconds between 1968 and 1972. Since the British athlete **Roger Bannister** broke the 4-minute mile barrier for the first time in history twenty years ago, many runners have beaten that time for the mile. The world's fastest miler is New Zealander **John Walker** whose time of 3:49·4 seconds at Gothenburg, Sweden, in August 1975 clipped 1·6 seconds off the previous record, held for only three months by the Tanzanian middle-distance runner **Filbert Bayi**.

The fastest speed sustained by a runner for one hour is 20·9km/h, achieved by the Netherlands long-distance athlete **Jos Hermens** in September 1975. But for stamina and sheer endurance the highest achievements are those of the following:

George Littlewood, an Englishman, who ran 1,003km at Madison Square Gardens, New

Jos Hermens

Joss Naylor

0·5	20	28	50		60
Tortoise	Man	Dragonfly	Rabbit		Greyhound

FASTEST runners

Wally Hayward

Roger Bannister breaking the 4-minute mile barrier.

John Walker

York, in 139 hours 1 minute (all within a six-day period) nearly a century ago.

South African **Wally Hayward**, who ran the equivalent of six marathons in 24 hours, an average speed of nearly 10*km/h*. The distance he covered was a fantastic 256*km*.

American **J. R. Beads**, who achieved the greatest non-stop run, 195*km*, in 1969. His time was 22 hours 27 minutes.

English fell-runner **Joss Naylor**, a Lake District farmer, who ran the 432*km* of the formidable Pennine Way, much of it over rough and mountainous country, in an incredible 3 days 4 hours 35 minutes in 1974. After this superhuman effort, Joss had a meal, slept for a couple of hours and then went home to milk his cows.

2	81	90	161 *km/h*
ox	Pronghorn	Cheetah	Spine-tailed swift

FASTEST shoepolishers...snake...bird...bat...centipede...desert drive

FOUR TEENAGERS POLISHED 4,314 pairs of shoes at Walsall, England, in 1974.

THE FASTEST LAND CROSS-ING of the Sahara Desert has probably been made not, as you might expect, by a profes-sional or a rally-driver, but by a top British rock drummer, Ginger Baker. He has driven across the Sahara no less than five times, and claims the fastest time — five days for the 3,200km journey from Cauta, Algeria, to Kano, Nigeria. An average of 640km a day for five consecutive days is good going on civilized roads — over desert 'roads', even allowing for the absence of traffic and other normal hazards, that time will take some beating.

THE FASTEST OF the 3,000 known species of centipede can keep up a speed of 7·2km/h, enough to beat a fast walker of the homo sapiens species. Having a few more legs probably helps! (However, it is a fallacy that centipedes usually have a hundred legs — some have more, many have fewer.)

THE AFRICAN BLACK MAMBA is probably the fastest-moving snake. Over a short distance it is reputed to be able to travel at *32km/h* downhill and *24km/h* on the level. The mamba is also among the ten most venomous snakes in the world.

THE FASTEST RECORDED FLIGHT by a bird is that of the aptly-named spine-tailed swift from Asia. A carefully monitored test was carried out in the U.S.S.R. during World War II and the astonishing figure that emerged was *171km/h*. Nor was the swift cheating, but flying level, not diving or swooping.

THE HIGHEST RECORDED FLYING speed for a bat is 51km/h by a free-tailed bat of New Mexico.

FASTEST flying insect...typist...shorthand-writer...barber

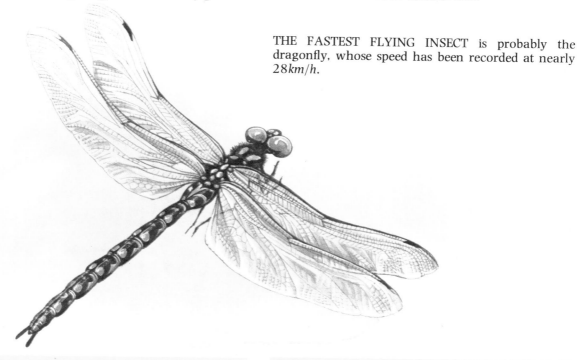

THE FASTEST FLYING INSECT is probably the dragonfly, whose speed has been recorded at nearly 28km/h.

THE FASTEST TYPIST on a manual machine was Margaret Owen, who reached the speed of 170 words per minute in New York as long ago as 1918. For endurance and speed, however, the winner is Albert Tangora, who kept up an average of 147 words per minute for one hour. Both were Americans using American machines. The equivalent 1-minute and 1-hour speeds for an electric typewriter are 216 and 149 wpm, both achieved by ladies.

BARBER GERRY HARLEY (*right*) shaved 130 men in an hour during a public demonstration in Kent, England in 1971.

THE FASTEST SHORTHAND SPEEDS are 300 wpm for 5 minutes and 350 wpm for 2 minutes, both achieved by an American, Nathan Behrin, in New York over fifty years ago.

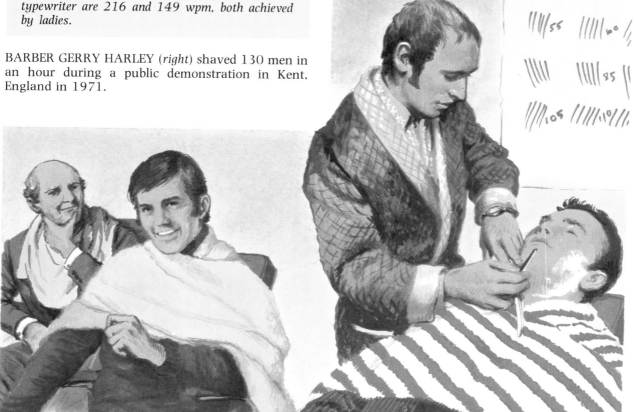

PROBABLY THE FASTEST long-distance backwards walk is 84km in 14 hours achieved by Lindsay Dodd, a 19-year-old Englishman, in 1974. This is 6km/h or a brisk forward walking speed for an experienced rambler, who would regard 84km as a very good day's walk indeed.

But the greatest backwards walker of all time must be the Texan, Plennie Wingo, who walked backwards for the 12,874km he covered while crossing whole continents during the early 1930s. It took him eighteen months to cover that distance.

THE EXPRESS LIFT (elevator) in the Sears Tower, Chicago, U.S.A. (*right*) is the fastest domestic passenger lift in the world. It travels to the 103rd floor at a speed of over 32km/h.

THE FASTEST-BUILT OFFICE BLOCK could well be the seven-storey one erected by a German building firm in Hamburg's city centre in 1970. The time for the complete job: 65 hours, 41 minutes, 23 seconds.

THE MOLE is probably the fastest tunneller: it can manage 68m in a single night.

FASTEST crab...ball game...bowler... manmade objects...Channel swim

THE FASTEST BALL GAME is *pelota*, of which the master exponents are the French and especially the Basques, for whom it is a national sport akin to cricket for the English. The ball, flung against a distant wall by means of a *chistera*, the curved hollow bat used for both catching and hurling, can reach speeds of up to 250*km/h*.

A 25-YEAR-OLD BRITON, Barry Watson, holds the record for the fastest English Channel crossing by a swimmer. He swam the 33km from Cap Gris-Nez, France to St Margaret's Bay near Dover, England in 9 hours 35 minutes in 1964. The record has stood for over ten years but it is a mere minute faster than the time taken by a 16-year-old American girl, Lynne Cox, for the England-to-France crossing in 1973. Lynne's time is the fastest by a woman and the fastest ever for the England/France direction.

THE SPEED RECORD for crabs is unofficially held by a conspicuously marked female sprinter who covered 20km in 23 days — just under 900m a day — in 1962.

DENNIS LILLEE AND JEFF THOMSON, the present whirlwind bowlers of the Australian Test team, are fast but do not have the speed of Harold Larwood, famous England Test bowler of the 'thirties, terror of the Australian batsmen of the time, and fastest bowler in cricketing history. Larwood could deliver a ball at nearly 160*km/h*.

Harold Larwood, now seventy, is alive and well and living contentedly among his old cricketing enemies in Sydney, Australia.

IN JANUARY 1975 a team of scientists from Birmingham, England, claimed to have achieved the fastest speed reached by an earthbound object. This was a carbon-fibre rod set up in their laboratory to test the effect of molecules in high-speed collision. The speed reached by the tip of the rod rotating in a vacuum was calculated to be 7,200km/h, about six times the speed of sound. The previous speed record for an earthbound object was 4,800km/h achieved in Pennsylvania, U.S.A. during the mid-1960s.

The fastest speed attained by an earth-launched space vehicle was over 173,000km/h when the American Pioneer II *passed the planet Jupiter in December 1974 en route to Saturn.*

FASTEST on land

THERE ARE FIVE RECOGNIZED 'fastest on land' records, classified according to the type of vehicle and the power source. The three main records are held by American drivers. The most important is the official 'absolute' world land speed record: 1,016 *km/h*, achieved by Gary Gabelich in his rocket-powered *Blue Flame* on Bonneville Salt Flats, Utah, U.S.A., in October 1970. The record for jet-engined cars is held by Craig Breedlove, who reached 988 *km/h* in *Spirit of America* (*right*) in November 1965, also at Bonneville. The same month and the same place saw the third world record set by an American, Bob Summers, when he reached 673 *km/h* in *Goldenrod*, a piston-engined car. The fourth world record, this time for a production car, belongs to a 4·9-litre 917L Porsche which touched 380 *km/h* at Le Mans in April 1971.

Finally the British speed king, the late Donald Campbell, is still credited with the fastest speed for a wheel-driven vehicle (that is, one with four wheels in parallel like a conventional car): 690 *km/h* in *Bluebird* at Lake Eyre, Australia, in July 1964.

There is also a sixth land speed record, not officially recognized. In December 1954 Lt Col John Stapp (U.S. Air Force) reached 1,011 *km/h* in a sled running on steel rails set up in the New Mexico desert.

The next target for the land-speed specialists is the penetration of the sound barrier, in other words, to travel faster than the speed of sound (1,184 *km/h*). It is reported that not only the Americans but also the Russians, British and Australians are working on

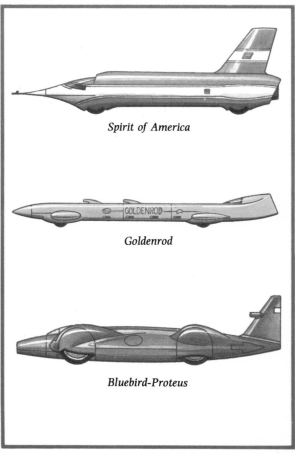

Spirit of America

Goldenrod

Bluebird-Proteus

FASTEST on water

designs for a vehicle capable of breaking the sound barrier on land.

Official records were first recognized at the turn of the century. A French count set the first, 68km/h, in 1898. For two decades France was supreme. Britain then took over until the early 1960s, when American drivers began – and still continue – to monopolize world speed records.

Donald Campbell, son of the famous speed king of the 1930s, Sir Malcolm Campbell, was killed when his turbo-jet boat *Bluebird K7* overturned while he was attempting a new world water-speed record on Coniston Water, England's Lake District, in January 1967. As he did not complete the two runs necessary for record recognition, he failed in his attempt on an official record. In the course of that last, tragic run he achieved the fastest speed ever reached on water, 527km/h.

The official world water-speed record (based on the average of two one-mile runs) of 459km/h is held by Lee Taylor Jr. of Downey, California, U.S.A. It was achieved in the hydroplane *Hustler* (*below*) on Lake Guntersville, Alabama, U.S.A. in June 1967, six months after Campbell's death.

The propeller-driven craft world speed record is 325km/h established by Larry Hill in his supercharged hydroplane *Mr Ed* at Long Beach, California, U.S.A.

FASTEST cyclist...trains...vehicle on rails

DR ALLAN ABBOTT, of California, U.S.A., reached the fastest speed attained by a cyclist at Bonneville Salt Flats, Utah, U.S.A., in August 1973. Riding behind a Chevrolet car fitted with a special windscreen, over a kilometre distance he reached the astonishing speed of 226km/h.

THE WORLD SPEED RECORD for a train is 376km/h, achieved by an American loco on a 9km test track in Colorado, U.S.A. in March 1974. The equivalent for a steam train is 202km/h. That was attained in 1938 and is hardly likely to be beaten because steam trains have been largely superseded by diesel oil and electric in most major countries of the world. The record-breaker was a train hauled by the famous British loco *Mallard* in 1938.

The Japanese run the fastest regular rail service in the world. Their National Railway trains (*below*) cover the 180km Osaka/Okayama run in exactly one hour, the 16-coach train reaching a maximum speed of 250km/h. The Tokyo/Osaka service is only slightly less speedy, the scheduled time for the much longer run of 515km being 3 hours 10 minutes – an average speed of 162km/h.

THE FASTEST SPEED ever reached on rails is attributed to an unmanned rocket-powered sled. On a 10km-long track in New Mexico, U.S.A. in 1959 it touched 4,900km/h or, in aircraft terms, Mach 4 – four times the speed of sound.

FASTEST swimmers...aircraft

WHAT FAMOUS AMERICAN FILM-STAR was also the world's fastest swimmer, an Olympic gold medallist in the early 1920s? The answer is Johnny Weissmuller, the first, best-known and, for many older film fans, the finest screen Tarzan.

He had a fantastic sprint style and speed, so every Tarzan film he appeared in had to include a sequence where he hurtled through the jungle river to rescue a damsel in distress from being eaten by an alligator.

How does he compare with the world's fastest swimmer today, the incredible Mark Spitz, winner of nine Olympic gold medals for the USA? Mark's 100m world-record time is 51·22 seconds, over six seconds faster than Johnny's half a century ago. That's what training, technique and, perhaps, greater competitiveness will do for human achievement.

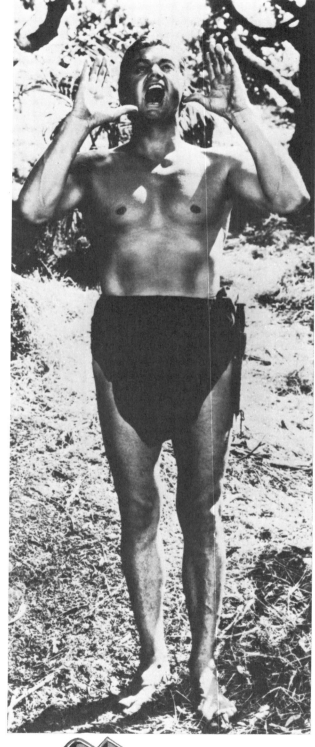

While Mark Spitz (*above*) is the world freestyle 100m record-holder, with a speed for the 100m of 7km/h, another American swimmer, David Edgar, was timed at 20·23 seconds over a length of 45·7m in an Alabama pool in March 1971. As that represents a speed of 8·12km/h, the fastest swimmer over *less* than the minimum Olympic distance is David Edgar.

THE FASTEST SPEED flown by a pilot of a fixed-wing aircraft is 7,297km/h, attained by Major W. Knight of the US Air Force in North American Aviation's experimental X-15A-2 in 1967.

THE LOCKHEED YF-12A (*below*) is the aircraft in which U.S. Air Force pilots Col R. Stephens and Lt Col D. Andre set up the official world air speed record. In May 1965 they achieved a speed of 3,331km/h over a short course (15–25km) in California, U.S.A.

FASTEST Wild West mail service

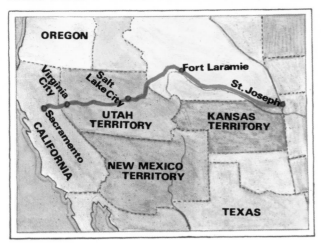

IN THE MIDDLE OF THE nineteenth century, for just sixteen months, the fastest means of communication between the eastern and western states of America was the Pony Express. At the time of its formation early in 1860, a railway system was still just a dream for pioneers, the telegraph was in its early stages of development and the normal means of transport, the stagecoach, was slow and cumbersome. There *was* a stagecoach route from St Joseph Missouri, in the east to Sacramento, California, near the west coast, but it was a leisurely, roundabout one that the Pony Express set out to beat.

They blazed a new but rough and hazardous trail between these two key centres by striking across desert and mountain, and over dangerous terrain, including Indian country. By cutting corners, as it were, Pony Express beat the stagecoach by days. Five hundred of the best horses and two hundred of the finest riders — most of them barely out of their teens — were recruited to see that the mails got through, come what may. Riders defied attacks by Indians, wolves and panthers, blizzards and other natural hazards that were to be met along the Pony Express route from St Joseph to Sacramento.

Once a week at first, then twice, the relays of horses and daredevil riders covered the 190-station,

3,200*km* journey in about ten days. The cost of sending mail by Pony Express was $5 for every 14*g* and $3.50 for a ten-word telegram. The fastest run was recorded in November 1860 when the news of President Lincoln's election was carried from Fort Kearny, Nebraska, to Fort Churchill, Nevada, in only six days.

But the days of the Pony Express were by then already numbered. By the summer of 1861 the fast-expanding Western Union Telegraph Company had established trans-continental telegraph lines to link east and west, enabling news to be transmitted far more quickly. The impatient Western newspapers thrived on news and wanted it fast, much faster than the 400*km*-a-day maximum the stretched Pony Express could offer. So a courageous enterprise was inevitably overtaken by scientific progress. Sixteen months after its opening, Pony Express closed with a total loss of $200,000. The new communications

FASTEST mail service in irregular use

system could make a much better, if far less exciting, job of linking east and west than the strained muscles and physical courage of brave men and horses. But a legend had been created in those sixteen months. The Pony Express and two folk heroes who rode in its service, 'Buffalo Bill' Cody and 'Wild Bill' Hickok, are remembered today as a stirring chapter in the history of the Wild West.

WHILE THE PONY EXPRESS was probably for that limited period the fastest scheduled long-distance postal service, a faster one had been operated from time to time for something like two thousand years, though never on a commercial basis. This service, the 'pigeon post', was set up only when required, sometimes just for one special task, and might be described as the fastest mailing method in irregular use.

The homing pigeon is not by any means the fastest bird. Indeed, it is well down the speed stakes with its top speed − on level flight and without wind-assistance − of about 90km/h. But it can be trained, and it does have an astonishing ability to find its way back home over great distances. (The longest homing flight on record is an estimated 11,265km − but that was exceptional.) This uncanny

Winky, and the award gained for his part in the rescue of a Beaufighter crew which crashed in 1942. They managed to release the bird with location details which it carried back to base.

Attaching a message to a carrier pigeon.

homing instinct has been known and exploited for ages. The Ancient Egyptians, Romans and Greeks all used the pigeon as a messenger, and it is reputed to have carried Olympic Games results to various cities in Ancient Greece. A pigeon postal service helped to save the blockaded city of Leyden, Holland, in the sixteenth century, carried war news at the time of Waterloo (1815), the 1848 revolution in Europe and both World Wars. One bird, called the Duke of Normandy, won the animals' V.C., the Dickin Medal (the highest British award for bravery), for his services with paratroops operating behind the German lines on D-Day during the Second World War.

Perhaps the most unusual and best-known use of pigeons as messengers occurred during the Siege of Paris in 1870−1. The city had been completely cut off from the outside world by the Prussian army, who had cut the only telegraph cable link with Paris. For five months the beleaguered city of two million

citizens and half a million garrison had no means of contact even with other parts of France, until an unusual form of postal service was organized. The French had been great balloonists ever since the first hot-air balloon flight had been made a century earlier, so some patriotic ballooning enthusiasts and pigeon-fanciers of Paris got together to thwart the Germans by organizing regular balloon/pigeon flights between the city and various parts of Europe. Nobody could blockade the air space. So up went the intrepid balloonists, floating over the heads of the enemy surrounding the city, risking German shell-fire, then at about 1800m setting their course for friendly territory. The service continued until Paris was relieved in January 1871. Official postal rates were fixed − 20 centimes for letters, and 10 for cards weighing up to 4g. On board the balloon, apart from mail and the occasional important person, would be a crate of homing pigeons (from a total of over a hundred) who would later fly vital messages back to their lofts inside the city.

FASTEST model aircraft... battleship... fish

THE MODEL-AIRCRAFT speed record is 343km/h, set up by two Russians with a radio-controlled plane in the Koktebel Valley, U.S.S.R., in September 1971. V. Gukin built it and V. Myakinin was the pilot. The same model also holds the world hydro record for model planes, 294km/h. It is shown (*right*) in its hydro form, equipped with floats for a water take-off.

THE FASTEST WARSHIP in service is the Royal Canadian Navy's 180-tonne hydrofoil sub-chaser *Bras d'Or*. Off Halifax, Nova Scotia, in July 1969, it reached a speed of 61 knots (*112km/h*).

THE SPEED RECORD for fish is easily held by the sailfish, with a maximum recorded speed of more than 100km/h. The second fastest and a long way behind is the marlin with 80km/h. The flying fish, which *sounds* as though it ought to be top of the speed table, is well down the list with a relatively slow speed of around 50km/h. For comparison, the fastest sealion or seal can manage a top speed of 40km/h. At the other extreme, the fastest seahorse is flat out at ·02km/h.

FASTEST speakers... knockouts... submarine

Above: **Raymond Glendenning, a famous radio voice of the 'fifties.**

IT IS DIFFICULT TO SPEAK English very fast and enunciate the words clearly enough to be understood for more than a very short time. Few people can keep up a speed of 300 words or more per minute for more than about half a minute. Perhaps the fastest recorded speed for speaking in English was the 436 words per minute achieved in a BBC television series called *Record Breakers* by Dr Charles Hunter of Rochdale, Lancs., England. He took just 36 seconds to recite the whole of the famous Hamlet soliloquy 'To be or not to be', 262 words in all. A well-known BBC radio commentator, the late Raymond Glendenning, was an extremely fast – and clear – talker familiar to British listeners. He once crammed a 176-word commentary on a dog race into 30 seconds. That's fast, yet still well behind Dr Hunter's record. Probably the fastest English-speaking international figure was the American President John Kennedy. In a 1961 speech he managed 327 words per minute for a short time.

To appreciate how fast these speaking speeds are, see how many words you can read quickly and clearly in one minute.

THE FASTEST RECORDED KNOCK-OUT in boxing history occurred in Maine, U.S.A. in 1946: $10\frac{1}{2}$ seconds. As this included the count (10 seconds), plainly either the timing was inaccurate or the successful boxer left his corner before the bell. So perhaps credit for the fastest KO should be given instead to Jerry 'The Blaster' Dorrough who knocked out Jan Smith with the first and only blow of the bout in a Golden Gloves event at Dallas, Texas, U.S.A. in January 1958. Even allowing for a slow count, the fight lasted just 18 seconds.

The fastest world heavyweight title fight KO occurred in Dublin, Ireland, in 1908 when Canadian Tommy Burns knocked out Jem Roche in 1 minute 28 seconds. Almost as fast was the 1 minute 52 second knock-out of the late 'Sonny' Liston by the reigning heavyweight champion of the world, Muhammad Ali, at Lewiston, Maine, U.S.A. in May 1965.

Though for the fastest world heavyweight title KO Ali must take second place to a boxer born nearly a century ago, most boxing experts would undoubtedly vote him the fastest heavyweight of all time. Ali himself, of course, would want to add 'the greatest', and most people would probably go along with that, too.

Below: **Muhammad Ali in action against Henry Cooper (1966).**

THE FASTEST SUBMARINE is the U.S. Navy's nuclear Skipjack class, capable of submerged speeds of 45 knots (83km/h).

THE FASTEST TIME recorded for smashing a piano into small enough pieces to pass through a 22·8cm-diameter hoop is 2 minutes 26 seconds. The feat, which included the time taken to pass the bits through the hoop, was achieved by an Irish team of six in 1968 using implements. The record for using bare hands only is held by a karate team of three men in Guernsey, C.I., who smashed a piano in 14 minutes.

In June, 1972, a 15-strong karate team from Bradford, Yorkshire demolished a six-roomed house in 6 hours using only their heads, feet and hands.

THE FASTEST SPEED attained on skis is 189km/h by Steve McKinney, a twenty-year-old American from Kentucky, in Italy in July 1974. The water-skiing speed record is also held by an American, Danny Churchill, who touched 202km/h in 1971. To complete the American clean sweep of the ski-speed titles, Sally Younger became the fastest woman water-skier in 1970 when she achieved 169km/h. Both records were set in California, U.S.A.

THE FASTEST EATING RECORDS include 27 dough-nuts in 7 minutes 16 seconds, 1,823 baked beans (cold, eaten singly with a stick) in 30 minutes, 13 raw eggs in 3·8 seconds and 130 prunes in 105 seconds.

THE TOUR DE FRANCE is the world's toughest, oldest, longest and most celebrated bicycle race. Every summer about 150 of Europe's best distance-riders attempt this 4000km cycling marathon, only half of them likely to finish. For three weeks, with only two rest days, the riders face a daily average of 200km in temperatures which can vary from 0° to 32°C and conditions of scorching sun or torrential rain. In the Alps and Pyrenees are gruelling climbs of up to 2,500m. Down the mountain roads riders may touch speeds of around 100km/h. The fastest average speed over the entire course was that of the legendary Jacques Anquetil of Normandy, five times winner, who averaged 37·3km/h in the 1962 Tour. None of his famous successors, even the great Eddy Merckx of Belgium, also five times winner, has improved on that.

FASTEST journeys round the earth...space travel

AROUND THE WORLD IN EIGHTY DAYS is the title of a well-known novel by the French writer Jules Verne and of a popular film based on the book. In the last century that was a very fast trip indeed. Nowadays less than three days is enough for the feat. The fastest round-the-world trip using commercial flights was 65 hours 58 minutes, achieved by an Australian, Gordon Banks, in June 1973.

THE FASTEST MAN HAS TRAVELLED is $39,897 km/h$. This speed was reached by astronauts Stafford, Cernan and Young (*right*) in *Apollo 10* on 26 May 1969. The *Apollo 10* mission had a special significance in the series of moon shots because it was the reconnaissance trip that prepared the way for the first moon landing later the same year (July 1969). None of the *Apollo 10* crew touched the moon's surface.

While Young remained in the command module (nicknamed 'Charlie Brown'), orbiting at a height of $100 km$, Stafford and Cernan in the lunar module ('Snoopy') traversed the moon's surface at $15,200 m$ to have a good look at the landing site chosen for *Apollo 11*.

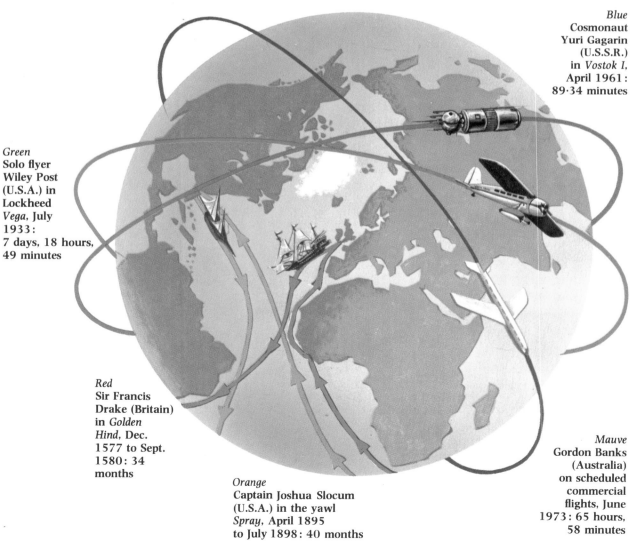

Blue
**Cosmonaut
Yuri Gagarin
(U.S.S.R.)
in *Vostok I*,
April 1961:
89·34 minutes**

Green
**Solo flyer
Wiley Post
(U.S.A.) in
Lockheed
Vega, July
1933:
7 days, 18 hours,
49 minutes**

Red
**Sir Francis
Drake (Britain)
in *Golden
Hind*, Dec.
1577 to Sept.
1580: 34
months**

Orange
**Captain Joshua Slocum
(U.S.A.) in the yawl
Spray, April 1895
to July 1898: 40 months**

Mauve
**Gordon Banks
(Australia)
on scheduled
commercial
flights, June
1973: 65 hours,
58 minutes**

Strangest

STRANGEST nautical mystery

JUST BEFORE CHRISTMAS a little over a century ago, Captain Morehouse, skipper of the brig *Dei Gratia* bound for Gibraltar, saw a strange ship approaching on the port bow. Through his telescope he could read the name: *Mary Celeste*. There was nothing strange about that for he knew the ship and her master, Captain Briggs, well enough. What puzzled him was why so experienced a skipper should sail on a port tack with sails set for starboard. That was not only strange — it was unbelievable. So, too, was the complete absence of crew on deck. There was not a sign of life anywhere. The *Celeste* was shrouded in silence and might have been a ghost ship. Had the crew taken to the lifeboat? Was it mutiny? Had there been some catastrophic event like an explosion? Was the crew lying dead below . . . or just drunk? There was one way to find out: board the *Celeste* and investigate. So Captain Morehouse and a boarding party carried out a thorough search of the ship. Several hours later they were even more baffled. Everything on the *Celeste* was in good order. Cooking utensils were stacked neatly in the galley, the cabins were tidy and the ship's cargo of 1,700 barrels of alcohol intact. The *Celeste* looked as spick and span as Captain Morehouse would have expected. But where was the crew? Of them and Captain Briggs, his wife and daughter — who were sailing with him on this voyage — there was no sign. The last entry in the log book had been made on 25 November, so for ten days the *Celeste* had apparently drifted at the mercy of the seas, without a soul aboard, living or dead.

Later, in Gibraltar, a Board of Enquiry was set up to investigate the mystery of the *Mary Celeste*. After a detailed survey of the ship, the experts could find no explanation for the disappearance of everyone on board. No evidence of fire, explosion, mutiny, violence, indeed anything unusual was discovered. All the experts could suggest, based on the fact that one of the 1,700 barrels had been opened, was that the crew had become crazed with drink and in an alcoholic stupor had murdered their captain and his family, flung them overboard and then made off in the ship's boat. They were all drowned, thought the experts, or perhaps had reached some remote shore, which would explain why nothing had been heard of them. But few people believed the official story.

STRANGEST animal trick...shell...mulish behaviour...sextet

The years went by but no clues, no bodies, no survivors, no news that had any bearing on the mystery turned up. There were many more theories, some of them fanciful, while some were quite ridiculous. One of the more plausible solutions was put forward at the time of the official investigation, though not by the experts. According to this theory, the 1,700 barrels of alcohol might have given off a highly inflammable gas which threatened to blow up the ship. Alarmed by the prospects, Captain Briggs had given the order to abandon ship. Everyone took to the boats which later capsized and all the occupants were drowned.

Although this theory is rather more convincing, it remains just a theory. Not a single clue to the fate of those on board the *Celeste* has ever come to light. Nothing was heard or seen of Captain Briggs, his family or crew again. The mystery of the *Mary Celeste* remains to this day one of the most baffling in seafaring history.

LATE IN 1975 near Chernigov, N. Ukraine, Russian archaeologists found a 20,000-year-old six-piece ensemble including drums and a xylophone made from the tusks and bones of mammoths.

LOOK CAREFULLY at the next dogwinkle (or periwinkle) you find on the shore. You'll see that from the top or point of the shell the twirls go in a right-handed or clockwise direction. Only about one in a million winkles have a left-handed twirl. Should you come across one, take it to a museum: it will be a very rare specimen indeed.

'WILY' AND 'CUNNING' are words often used to describe the fox, regarded as one of the shrewdest of wild animals. Apparently the rat is no idiot, either. Farmers used to be baffled by the disappearing-egg trick performed by rats, which are undoubtedly adept at stealing hens' eggs. Tell-tale broken shells by their run a long way from the hen's nest proved that rats were the culprits. But how did they manage to carry eggs any distance without breaking them?

Many a countryman was mystified by the feat. But one day somebody caught the thieves in the act and the secret was out. The rats worked in pairs, one lying on its back holding the egg firmly but gently between its paws, the other pulling its accomplice along by the tail as though it were a cart. Now what bright rat worked that out and how did the word get around the rat world?

But 12,480 not-so-bright rats were killed by a London tabby cat called Minnie during a six-year reign of terror between 1927 and 1933.

IN DENVER, COLORADO, mules were used to haul trams uphill. They were allowed to ride on the rear platform for the return, downhill journey. A local farmer bought one of these animals for ploughing and had great difficulty in persuading it to walk down any hilly field. It wanted to hitch a lift on the plough.

STRANGEST unidentified flying object

'UFO' (UNIDENTIFIED FLYING OBJECT) is the term used to describe anything moving in the sky that cannot be identified as either of human origin, such as an aircraft, or a natural phenomenon like a meteor. In recent years, thousands of UFO sightings in various parts of the world have been recorded, inspiring theories, some very strange stories, and several books. Typical reports, some from 'eye-witnesses' with stronger-than-average imaginations, describe the activities of flying saucers and strange beings from outer space, but most people take these stories with a pinch of salt, in the absence of real evidence.

There is no doubt, however, that UFOs occur. Many experienced and intelligent people who are not easily misled — such as policemen and airline pilots — have recorded UFO sightings.

Some have been seen by more than one eye-witness, some photographed. All reports are investigated, scientifically studied and officially recorded. Many have been authenticated and no reasonable explanation for the happening has been put forward.

One eye-witness in Beverley, Mass., U.S.A. reported: 'It was like a luminous platter hovering over the school. I heard no sound at all, but I felt this thing was going to come down on top of me. It was like a giant mushroom.'

Two police officers were summoned to the scene. One said: 'I observed what seemed to be a large plate hovering over the school. It had three lights, red, green and white — but no noise to indicate it was a plane. This object hovered over the school and appeared almost to stop. The lights were flashing. The object went over the school twice and then went away.'

This was in fact a multiple sighting — that is, several people in different places saw the UFO simultaneously. The sighting lasted 45 minutes altogether. It was just one among hundreds of similar cases, all of them defying explanation.

Another experienced observer, an air-traffic controller, saw an object orbiting on the edge of an air force base runway. The object disappeared at speed but was picked up on radar and remained on his screen for twenty minutes. No aircraft was in the vicinity and there was no reasonable explanation for the mysterious object.

A faked photograph of a UFO sighting. *Alfred Gescheidt*

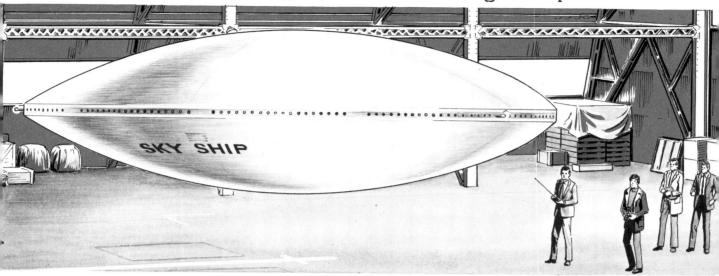

A GENUINE FLYING SAUCER was sighted by a number of reliable eye-witnesses in an old hangar near Bedford, England, on 17 April 1975. They watched the 10*m*-diameter monster take off, dive and carry out various impressive manoeuvres at very low altitudes, almost at ground level in fact. This flying saucer — it could be called an Identified Flying Object — was a helium-filled, radio-controlled and battery-powered scale model of a skyship, the brain-child of an inventor who hopes that his version of the flying saucer will one day become a commercial craft capable of carrying about 400 tonnes of freight 6,400*km* without refuelling. The *Skyship* would be cargo- not passenger-carrying, and each one would cost up to £20,000,000. The full-scale commercial version will be 240*m* in diameter, 62*m* deep and will be driven by ten gas-powered turbo-prop engines. It will fly at a maximum height of 1,500*m* and an average speed of 160*km/h*.

So if in a few years' time you see somewhere a vast flying saucer coming in to land, it is more likely to be filled with a consignment of boots, bulldozers or one of a thousand other man-made, down-to-earth articles than with little green men from Outer Space.

WHAT MUST SURELY BE the only monument in the shape of a seagull may be seen at Salt Lake City, Utah, U.S.A. The tall, imposing monument honoured the bird for a service it once did for the State. Utah had been overrun by a colossal hoard of grasshoppers which moved mercilessly across the country, devouring every living green thing in sight. Farmers despaired for their crops and ruin faced the state of Utah. Then came a huge flock of seagulls from the Pacific which ate the hoards of grasshoppers until not one remained. The monument in Salt Lake City, topped by a man-sized seagull, was the people's way of remembering their saviours.

AN ENORMOUS EXPLOSION in a remote Siberian forest in 1908 was caused, scientists believed until recently, by a giant meteorite. In 1975 came an amazing new theory — that a $\frac{3}{4}$km-diameter snowball weighing 1 million tonnes hurtled from space hitting the earth's atmosphere at 40,000km/h.

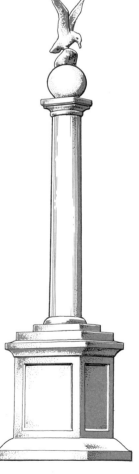

ONCE IT WAS NOT uncommon to see guns made with muzzles resembling the wide-open mouths of fierce animals, but this bronze mortar, made in the eighteenth century for Tipu Sahib, Sultan of Mysore, is a rarity. It is shaped and decorated to look like a tiger, an animal for which the sultan had a great passion.

STRANGEST journey to the sun

MOST BIRDS MIGRATE, even the young. There is no mystery about *why* they do. They go to search for a more favourable climate and to avoid the over-crowding of their native breeding grounds: these are just two reasons. Some small, hardy birds that need little food can survive an Arctic winter and have no need to migrate. But it is a mystery how they manage to find their way to their new homes, perhaps a continent away, across oceans and mountain ranges and through all kinds of weather conditions.

What sort of system do they use to find the same winter quarters, year after year? Man can do no more than guess. Although there are theories and clues there is no generally accepted explanation. Do they take bearings on sun, moon or stars like ancient mariners? Have they some kind of 'radar' that homes in on the earth's magnetic fields? Does the strength of the wind in each direction have any significance? Or do they respond to landmarks, familiar features they can see on the ground?

Storms, or heavy cloud over the sea, can send them off course, though the distraction is only temporary and they soon pick up the correct course again. Migration is not a hurried business. Most birds take their time and fly for spells of a few hours only at low altitudes of around 900*m*, generally at night when it is safer.

The greatest distance covered by a migrant is 22,400*km*. The record-holder is an Arctic tern, like the one shown above, ringed as a nestling in July 1955 at a bird sanctuary about 200*km* from Murmansk, U.S.S.R., and captured alive by a fisherman

Arctic tern, and the main routes taken by migrating birds.

near Fremantle, Western Australia, in May of the following year. Another remarkable flight by the same breed of 17,600*km*, from Greenland to South Africa, was made by a bird, only four months old when it left home, in under four months' travelling time. In other words, the young tern had flown on average over 1,000*km* a week.

The tern has remarkable stamina and endurance but other birds have undertaken long flights and challenged the tern's achievements. For example, in 1966 a Manx shearwater flew from Wales, U.K., to Australia, a distance of 19,200*km*, in six months. That same year a mallard from Peterborough, England, reached Canada by the Siberia route only to be shot on reaching Alberta, a sad fate indeed after an epic journey of 16,000*km*. The albatross is also a marathon migrant: it flies round the world in eighty days between breeding seasons, covering some 30,000*km*.

Left: **wild ducks, which fly in a V-formation when migrating, take off in a flock from the ground.**

STRANGEST mass exodus

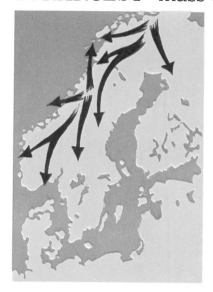

Above: the Norwegian lemmings' migration routes.

Right: lemmings on the move, in the film *White Wilderness. Walt Disney Productions*

BIRDS ARE NOT THE ONLY MIGRANTS: other animals also have a strange urge at certain times to leave their natural breeding grounds and move to new territory perhaps hundreds of miles away.

One of the oddest of the ground migrants is the Norwegian lemming, a small, stubby-tailed rodent about 15*cm* long which normally lives in burrows or rock crevices. A vegetarian, feeding on plants and roots, the lemming normally leads a dull, routine rodent life. Then it happens. Every few years, and for no known reason, the lemming gets that restless feeling . . . This happens after a season of over-breeding, when the colony becomes overcrowded. One pair of lemmings can produce as many as fifty offspring in a year and when a population 'explosion' occurs there are too many lemmings chasing too little food. Lemmings also apparently suffer from a form of claustrophobia, a fear of being closed in, a terrifying feeling that can also affect humans.

When conditions become intolerable, the lemming feels the irresistible urge to move on. It isn't a mass decision: no lemming leader orders the marathon to begin. Each creature makes his own decision to leave his crowded home and set out on a long and perilous journey into the unknown.

Hundreds, sometimes thousands, follow their individual instinctive route rather than each other: there is nothing sheep-like about the movement. The determined scurrying of large numbers across the Norwegian landscape is a strange and awesome sight. Watching it, you would think an invisible Pied Piper was luring them on.

The lemmings move deliberately as though they were heading for a known destination, following perhaps some mystical 'radar beam'. Why they move at all, why they take the direction they do, what motivates them – all these factors are mysteries to man.

The migrants cover about 8*km* a day on average. They look for the easy way round or over obstacles they meet and will avoid water if they possibly can, though they can swim. They will seek ways of crossing rivers without getting wet, using fallen trees or ice or other means to reach the other side. If there really is no other way, they will take to the water and swim, even though in rough conditions they cannot survive for more than a short time. For many lemmings migration ends in tragedy. They are drowned or killed by enemies encountered on the way in strange, unfamiliar territory far from their home, while their companions continue deliberately onwards. Some reach the sea eventually and try to cross that too, with the inevitable result. There used to be a theory that the Norwegian lemmings were compelled by some weird death wish to head for the sea and there commit mass suicide, but this is not taken seriously by scientists today and the mystery of the lemmings remains.

STRANGEST convict...dental job

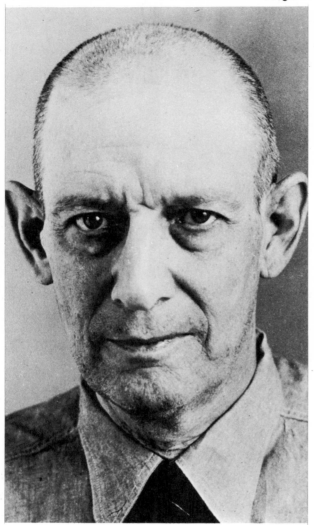

killed half his collection. He cured the others with crude but effective surgery using only a pocket-knife and his fingernail.

His power over humans as well as birds was demonstrated in 1946 when single-handed he quelled a mutiny on the notorious island prison of Alcatraz. off the coast of California.

He died in the prison hospital in Springfield, Missouri aged seventy-three. Soon after, Alcatraz was closed. It is now an adventure island and popular tourist attraction.

FOR A BIRD, LOSING or damaging a beak is a serious handicap, and if the beak is an outsize proboscis about a third the size of the bird's body, as in the case of a ten-year-old Great Indian Hornbill which broke its beak in an Isle of Man wildlife park, it could prove fatal. This bird was lucky: a dental technician was able to make a plastic beak after taking an impression of the broken one. While waiting for the new beak the helpless hornbill had to be force-fed, and ran the risk of pneumonia, for with no beak it could not reach its rear oil gland to preen its feathers and make them waterproof; but the new beak, screwed and glued in place, was successful and the bird survived.

ROBERT STROUD SPENT fifty-four years of his life in American prisons, forty-three of them in solitary confinement, for two murders. Although illiterate when he started his sentence at the age of eighteen, Stroud became an authority on bird behaviour, wrote a book on birds' diseases, studied astronomy, philosophy, logic and languages in prison and inspired the film *Birdman of Alcatraz* starring Burt Lancaster.

In 1908 the man who was later to become one of America's most celebrated convicts was jailed for the manslaughter of a man whom he shot for beating up his girlfriend. During his lifetime in prison, four campaigns for his release and a petition containing 100,000 signatures were organized, all to no avail. His fate was sealed when after serving forty years, he killed a brutal warder and was sentenced to death. From his cell window he watched the gallows being erected. However, a last-minute appeal succeeded, and his sentence was commuted to life imprisonment.

His passion for birds began when a sparrow flew into his cell. He soon had a small aviary of birds housed in cages he built himself. His influence on birds was uncanny. He taught them tricks which could be performed at the snap of his fingers. Once a fever

THE DESIGNER OF the 8,000cc *Gee Bee Super Sportster* wanted to pack the maximum power into the smallest possible airframe.

The result was this short, stubby aircraft that was little more than a flying engine, with the pilot's cockpit a sort of stuck-on afterthought at the tail end. This curious craft won a major trophy race in 1932 at a speed of 400km/h.

THERE HAVE BEEN SOME remarkable examples of dreams that have proved to be premonitions of events to come — usually disastrous and sometimes, but not always, affecting the dreamer. One of the most celebrated premonitions occurred to Abraham Lincoln, the great American president. While he and his wife were entertaining friends at the White House, he mentioned a dream he had experienced a few days earlier. The details, still vivid in his mind, had disturbed him.

'I dreamed I was walking through the White House,' he said, 'and as I walked I heard sobbing, though I could see nobody. I went from room to room but could see not a living person, yet the mournful sounds followed me. When I entered the East Room I saw a dais on which rested a corpse in funeral vestments. Soldiers stood around, acting as guards, and a throng of people gazed at the corpse, whose face I could not see as it was covered. "Who is dead in the White House?" I demanded. "The President", replied a soldier. "He was killed by an assassin." Then came a loud burst of grief from the crowd which woke me from my dream.' A few days later at ten o'clock on the night of Good Friday, 1865, Lincoln was killed by an assassin's bullet as he sat in a theatre box in Washington.

STRANGEST pirate stories

Kydd conducted a highly successful campaign, capturing a number of ships in the service of France. But when he arrived in New York, with ninety bars of gold among his booty, he was arrested for piracy. He was later executed – not for being a pirate, but for killing a mutineer with a bucket. The cost of the bucket, 8d (3½p), was carefully recorded on the charge sheet. (Such a punishment was not unusually harsh by the standards of the day: even a trivial theft could warrant death, or at best a merciless flogging.)

Left: Captain Kydd was executed for killing a mutineer with a bucket.

Above: Henry Morgan was, as well as being a notorious pirate, also Governor of Jamaica.

CAPTAIN KYDD WAS ONE of the best known and most successful pirates of all time. The son of a Scottish preacher, he became captain of a privateer towards the end of the seventeenth century. He was a legalized (as opposed to a private-enterprise) pirate: in those days privateers were authorized by the government to seek and destroy the ships of England's enemies. Any profits from the sale of captured ships or loot found on board were shared by the privateer-owners with official approval.

The king of England, William III, gave Kydd, one of his favourite mariners, command of the privateer *Adventure*. Though strictly a pirate himself, and a ruthless one too, Kydd was ordered by the king to stop the piracy that was rife around the American coast. It was being carried out largely by the French, then at war with England, so the government was all the more anxious to stamp it out. For that reason, they set a thief to catch a thief.

Henry Morgan, one of the most notorious pirates that ever sailed the seas, was knighted by King Charles II of England and made Governor of Jamaica. This came about because the Spaniards claimed the whole of the West Indies at the time and had driven out the tough white islanders who raised cattle there to sell to passing ships. These exiles turned to piracy, raided Spanish-occupied towns and plundered Spanish ships for treasure. As long as no British ships were attacked, King Charles offered his support and protection to the pirates, eventually rewarding the most notorious of them with high honours. It was by no means every pirate who won a knighthood and governorship for his cut-throat services!

STRANGEST gifts...precaution...machine...colour sense...identification

FOR CENTURIES it was erroneously believed that man could make himself airborne using only the strength of his own body provided his flying machine was correctly designed — a mistake which even the great Leonardo made. In the nineteenth century, one cycling enthusiast decided that pedal-power might be the answer. He invented this weird contraption, the aerial cycle, in 1888. Needless to say it was a complete failure, having no possibility of becoming airborne without a proper engine (and even then, it could hardly be said to have aerodynamic styling!).

HANS CHRISTIAN ANDERSEN, the famous Danish storyteller of the nineteenth century, always carried a rope with him when he stayed in a hotel in case the place caught fire. The rope can still be seen in a Danish museum. He was so scared of being buried alive he sometimes left notes by his bedside while he slept which read 'I am not really dead'. He begged his friends to make quite sure he was dead by cutting an artery before putting him in the coffin. He couldn't bear the thought of waking up inside and finding he was still alive.

THE BRIGHT ORANGE PATCH round the ears is the only means a female King penguin has of identifying a male. When a group of males had their orange patches painted black in a scientific experiment, the poor things were completely ignored by all the females.

SAKOWITZ IS A department store in Houston, the space centre in Texas, the oil millionaires' state. In its Christmas catalogue the store offers some rather special unusual presents, which they call 'Gifts of Knowledge'. They include ten lessons from the world's top swimmer Mark Spitz, for £45,000: a week's instruction on space-craft flying from astronaut Walter Cunningham, for £26,000: and a game of tennis with champion John Newcombe, for a mere £3,500. Customers wanting something really cheap can learn to be a Hollywood stuntman for a mere £1,200. Or they can have the whole gift package, every lesson in the catalogue, for £325,000. The store is careful to point out that the cost of transport is extra.

STRANGEST monster... slimmers

Could it be 'Nessie'? This photo, by H. L. Cockrell, shows what might be just a floating stick: but floating sticks do not cause a wash . . .

Nessy has been investigated by various expeditions — including a Japanese team — over the years. Long-range cameras and deep-water sonic equipment have been used and 24-hour-manned observation posts set up, but no one has uncovered any evidence that Nessy exists.

What about the photograph mentioned above of the humped sea serpent? Scientists have explained that by a dozen theories ranging from a claim that the picture shows floating, peculiar-shaped vegetation or branches, to one that the camera was focused on a swimming otter with her family in line behind her representing the 'humps'. The photograph was, after all, taken some distance away from the object and not in ideal conditions, hence the rather vague, blurred image.

Nessy has inspired tens of thousands of words, spoken and written, from naturalists, biologists and other learned people with theories to offer or to condemn. Yet we are no nearer solving the mystery now than we were nearly half a century ago when the Loch Ness Monster was first sighted and recognized 'officially'.

LEGENDS ABOUT MONSTERS in deep lakes are quite common in Scandinavia but one of the best known stories of this kind comes from Scotland. The 137m-deep Loch Ness is one of the deepest lakes in Britain and its 'monster' has been a celebrity on and off since the early 1930s. Rather dim and distant photographs of 'Nessy' have been taken by eye-witnesses, one of them showing a raised, curved head and a series of humps on the surface of the loch. But then, there have also been photographs supposedly of 'flying saucers' — yet they are hardly good enough evidence to convince scientists.

SEVERAL THOUSAND LADIES in the United States of America have tried a novel way of slimming: they have had their jaws wired together to stop them eating solid food and thereby putting on weight. One lady who weighed 103kg before the treatment had her jaws 'locked' for seven months. Keeping her mouth shut meant she could neither eat nor talk, but she did lose 33kg as a result. To stay alive during the 'lockjaw' period, she sipped a liquid diet through her clenched teeth.

THE ABOMINABLE SNOWMAN — in Tibetan, the *yeti* — is a legendary monster reputed to inhabit the Himalayas above the snowline. Prints resembling a huge human foot have been found in the snow of the southern slopes. Experts believe the prints may have been made by bears or have some other explanation, but special expeditions to find evidence of the Snowman have been fruitless. The Sherpas, hardy mountain people of Nepal who have taken part in most Everest expeditions, firmly believe in the *yeti* and some claim to have seen the monster. But explorers from the West need convincing evidence before they will take the Snowman seriously.

GOLD USED FOR dental purposes has to be soft and workable. In America long ago, dentists used gold coins that had been softened by being placed on the railway track and left there until a train had run over them.

A NEWFOUNDLAND CENT STAMP issued in 1866 featured a picture of a seal on an ice floe. People thought the artist had made a silly mistake because he had depicted the seal with forefeet instead of flippers. Indeed, the stamp was reissued some years later with the seal's feet replaced by flippers.

For a long time the stamp was regarded as a rare example of an artist's error being passed for philatelic reproduction. It was not until well into the twentieth century that it was discovered that the artist was right after all — for the great grey seal, a very rare mammal, actually does have feet, not flippers, in front.

DURING JULY 1945 in Resguill, County Donegal, Ireland, shoals of herring rained from the sky and turned the streets into a sea of silver. No one knows what caused this freak of nature. Some people thought it was an ill omen but the wiser, less superstitious inhabitants rushed indoors for baskets to make the most of the heaven-sent gift.

FISH DIE OUT OF WATER so if a drought dries out their natural habitat they cannot survive. The African lungfish (*above*) has an ingenious way of overcoming this problem. If its home dries out, it wraps up in a cocoon of dried slime stored in the glands of its skin; this will keep its body moist for months or even years. The lungfish has gills and air bladders that work like a pair of lungs, so by pressing its eel-like body into a ball and putting its mouth to an air hole, it can pass the drought time sleeping. If necessary it can survive in this way for as long as five years, certainly until the next rainy season fills his pool again. When the rains come the cocoon of hard mud softens and the lungfish can wriggle back to the water.

EVER SEEN YOURSELF in a distorting mirror? That's the kind you come across in funfairs, those wavy, full-length mirrors that give you legs like stilts, a tiny flat head and an enormous, balloon-shaped body — or some other comic combination. It seems that all distorting mirrors are made by one East London firm, T. & W. Ide, a glassworks which has specialized in this odd form of funmaking for over a century.

STRANGEST plants

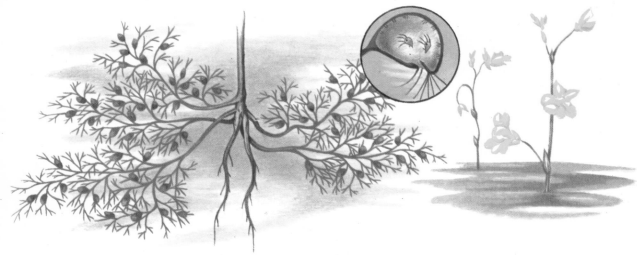

'CARNIVOROUS' MEANS FLESH-EATING, and the word is usually applied to animals, particularly the fierce big cats, and man. But there are carnivorous plants that are delicate and beautiful to look at, yet have the most vicious habits when it comes to catching their prey. For these plants are meat-eaters too, and need meat in order to live, just like the tiger, lion and other carnivores. All these sinister beauties grow in poor soil that lacks nitrogen, so essential to their survival. As the soil cannot provide the nitrogen, they get it from animals they catch, mostly insects, and they set the most ingenious traps to catch their unsuspecting prey. The beautiful Venus fly-trap, found on the eastern seaboard of the U.S.A., attracts its victims by its colour and the sweet nectar on the inside of each leaf. The oval leaves are hinged in pairs and have a row of sharp spikes along the outer edges. The insect, greedy for the nectar, walks across the hairy leaf. Two of the hairs – only two – when touched, trigger the trap's hinges and snap the jaws together like lightning. The insect is trapped behind the spiky 'bars' and cannot escape. The Venus absorbs the nitrogen-rich juices from its body and only discards the husk when the insect has been sucked dry. One marvellous feature of the Venus trap mechanism is that it can detect when the wrong food has been trapped and open up quickly. It can also detect raindrops: even if they touch the two trigger hairs they do not cause the trap to work.

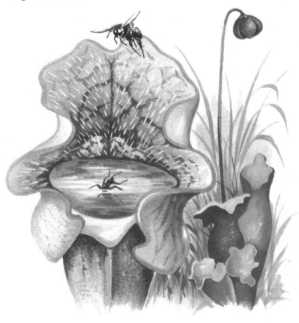

The bladderwort uses different but no less ingenious methods. It grows in boggy areas and on the surface it is simply a lovely yellow flower. Under the water, however, it trails a seaweed like a row of bladders, each no more than *2mm* in diameter, and filled with trapdoors with guide hairs that trigger the hinge mechanism when touched.

Another deadly killer is the pitcher plant, found in stagnant bogs in North America, and also Northern Ireland. Its long, hollow, horn-shaped leaves have no cunning trap mechanism like the other two. The pitcher relies on colour, nectar on its upper leaf, and a slippery surface like an ice glacier that takes the helpless dungfly or wasp (the pitcher's favourite diet) into the depths of the horn, where it is devoured.

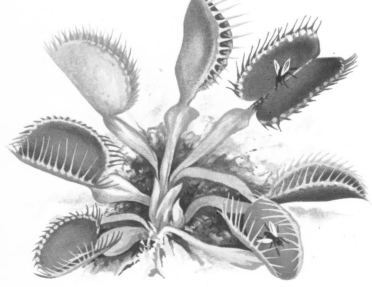

IN NATURE, THERE ARE some remarkable examples of camouflage. Among the animals and insects which, by their colouring and shape, blend with their background so well that they are almost invisible to their enemies even at close range, is the flower mantis. A common insect of India, it uses its superb camouflage as a deadly weapon, not to protect it from enemies but to snare its victims. The mantis has a hood behind the head which looks like a leaf and hind legs which look like petals. The top surface of its body is green, the underpart a pinkish violet, easily mistaken for the heart of an attractive flower.

When hungry, the mantis does not hunt for food. Instead it lies prone on the top of a rosebush until an unsuspecting butterfly, mistaking it for a flower, settles on or near it. Then the mantis lashes out with its front legs, which are cruelly barbed with rows of needle sharp spikes. If any part of the delicate butterfly is impaled on those deadly spikes, there is no hope of its escaping.

HANGING FROM THE ROOF of Waitomo Cave in New Zealand are thousands of tiny caterpillars which radiate an eerie blue light that is so bright it's possible to read a book by it. This light attracts flying insects that are then eaten by the caterpillars. They are extremely sensitive to sound, however, so if there is the slightest noise in the cave the lights are extinguished just as though an electric light had been switched off.

SOME WILD CREATURES are clever at looking after themselves when they're injured. The woodcock, for instance, will mould a cast from mud, roots and grasses to protect a broken leg. When the mud is dry and hard the bird can hop about quite happily until the leg mends and its protective cover can be pecked off.

THIRTY YEARS AFTER his mysterious disappearance, there is still worldwide enthusiasm for the distinctive style and recordings of Glenn Miller, famous American bandleader of the late 1930s. The Glenn Miller Orchestra was to dance music what the Beatles were to pop music two decades later.

His records sold in millions and there were — indeed still are — Miller fans all over the world. It was coming up to Christmas 1944 when Major Glenn Miller, then in Europe as director of the Army Air Forces band, took off from an English airstrip in a light plane. He planned to do the short trip across the Channel to France, much of which had by then been liberated by the Allies. Visibility was extremely poor, so much so that Miller remarked before the flight that 'even the birds are grounded today'. Nothing more was seen or heard of him. He, a colleague, the pilot and plane simply vanished without trace. Not a single clue to their fate ever came to light. Did he reach France? Did his plane come down in the Channel? Was he shot down by a stray enemy plane? Nobody knows. But his music, recordings and two films live on as a reminder to millions of one of the all-time greats in the history of popular music.

SOME SPECIES OF SPIDERS, among them small, innocent-looking house varieties, are cannibals. The female is larger than the male and after mating is very likely to attack her mate and have him for dinner. Not only will she eat her mate but her young too: out of an average 800 eggs laid by Mum, probably little more than ten per cent will survive as live spiders. Nor is she the only cannibal in the family: it has been discovered that the young of the most common spider in Britain, a species to be found in most cellars and garden sheds, sometimes eat their mothers alive.

The octopus has been known to be self-cannibalistic: that is, in certain rare but authenticated cases it has eaten itself. One case was reported by an aquarium in Germany: suddenly giving up its normal diet of fish and mussels, the octopus started chewing its own arms, continuing for several weeks until only the stumps of its eight arms remained. Not surprisingly the creature died, having literally eaten itself to death.

Left: **Glenn Miller, the bandleader of the 1930s whose music still enjoys enormous popularity today.**

THE POPULAR PHRASE 'to breed like flies' was well chosen. It has been estimated that if the offspring of just one pair of flies and their offspring for generations all survived and bred unchecked, after only one year the earth's entire surface would be covered with flies to a depth of 14m.

STRANGEST hen's egg ...tale of a dolphin

THE ARAUCANA HEN, a native of Chile but now popular as a pet in the U.S.A., is the only domestic hen to lay coloured eggs. While all other breeds lay white or brown, the Araucana uniquely produces eggs in attractive pastel shades of green, pink and blue. Once it has laid an egg of one particular colour, all the bird's other eggs will be the same colour, but it does not follow that a hen hatched from a blue egg will lay blue eggs: they could just as easily be green or pink.

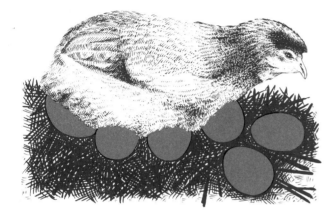

THE DOLPHIN, BECAUSE OF its jumping prowess, manoeuvrability, speed (up to 60km/h) and learning ability, has become for the public something of a circus act. 'Dolphinariums', where trained dolphins perform tricks, have sprung up all over the world. But long before the first trained dolphin appeared on the scene, one of its ancestors had become a famous figure — indeed, to thousands of mariners, a legend.

It was called Pelorus Jack and it inhabited the waters of Pelorus Sound and French Pass off the coast of New Zealand. This was a busy shipping route and Jack appointed himself voluntary guide and pilot to vessels using it. As a ship emerged from the sound, Jack would suddenly appear, take his place at the bow and, leaping and frolicking, lead the ship to the pass entrance. There it considered its job done, turned and went back to the sound to await the next arrival. The strange thing about Jack was his choosiness. He would not escort *any* ship, only some of the regular steam ships. He ignored sailing ships completely. This is odd, for whales — and dolphins are classified as whales — are not usually afraid of sailing ships, though they are of steamers, because the noise of the propeller scares them. But the courageous Jack was unafraid of the noise and for some mysterious reason preferred the throbbing steamer to the silent sailing ship.

During his years on escort duty, Jack became better known than most of the official, human pilots. Mariners loved Jack and greeted him as an old friend, as indeed he was. Although the friend of thousands, Jack was nevertheless hunted by a few determined wicked men intent on a kill. Jack succeeded in eluding them with the help of the New Zealand Government which passed an Order in Council giving special protection to Pelorus Jack and making it illegal to hunt him.

Once he got too adventurous, swam too near a ship and was hit. He retired injured for nine months, but reappeared when the wounds had healed to take up his old job. But he had learned a lesson; never again did he venture too close to a ship.

Jack's voluntary pilot duties continued through a quarter of a century. He did his first trip in 1889, his last in 1914. During the first year of World War I Jack disappeared, never to be seen again. By that time his body was a mass of scars from the claws and suckers of the cuttlefish that formed his main diet. What happened to him? Did he die of old age, was he attacked by some other creature or was he killed secretly by some poacher in spite of that Order in Council? Nobody knows. But one thing is certain: Jack was mourned by thousands of tough, New Zealand mariners when they realized they would never see again the sleek, streamlined shape come leaping through the waves to greet them. To them, Pelorus Jack had been a true friend of man.

IN RIVERDALE, A SUBURB of New York, a nineteen-storey block of flats with school, theatre, gymnasium, swimming pool and store incorporated has been built in reverse, that is, from the top *downwards*. First the 80*m* towers containing lifts and stairs were constructed. Each floor, complete with all fittings like pipes and even bathrooms, was put together on the ground and then hoisted at 8*m/h* into position by hydraulic jacks, starting with the *top* floor and working downwards to the ground.

The system used is a patented one that is claimed to be cheaper and quicker than the conventional bottom-to-top building method, offers better protection against earthquakes and does not need any of the usual paraphernalia like scaffolding or cranes. The Riverdale block of flats would have cost $1,000,000 more and taken up to nine months longer to complete if conventional building methods had been used.

IN ORDER TO PERFORM composer John Cage's 'orchestral' work 'First Construction in Metal' you need a piano with a metal rod laid on the strings, tubular and sleigh bells, eight cow bells, twelve oxen bells, five thunder sheets, four brake drums, four Turkish and four Chinese cymbals, three Japanese temple gongs, one suspended gong and four muted gongs, four muted anvils and a tam-tam.

THE FAMOUS LEANING BELL TOWER in the small Italian town of Pisa was started in 1174 but not completed until 1350. By then the angle of tilt of the 53*m* tower, which makes it look as if it is keeling over, was nearly 4*m*. By the early 1900s it was about 5*m* out of the perpendicular. During its construction the local inhabitants thought the tilt was deliberate but it is now believed that this developed accidentally, probably because the foundations are only 3*m* deep and do not extend beyond the wall perimeter. Some years ago a concrete platform was constructed at the base to prevent further tilting. Climbing the 293 steps of the tower is an eerie experience for it really does feel as though it's falling over.

Experts are divided about the fate of the tower, which tilts slightly more each year. Some think it will collapse in slow motion, as it were, over many years; others believe that a sudden movement in the unstable foundations of silt, sand and clay could be dangerous. The seventeenth-century English writer John Evelyn, after seeing the tower, wrote in his famous Diary: 'How it is supported from falling I think would puzzle a good geometrician.'

Over three hundred years later, the tower goes on leaning and still puzzles the experts, while continuing to be a major tourist attraction, despite its condition, bringing about a million visitors a year to Pisa.

THAT DELIGHTFUL LITTLE Australian animal, the koala bear, has one peculiar characteristic: it never drinks. The koala feeds on a species of eucalyptus tree that supplies it with both food and moisture. The koala, the real-life model for the traditional teddy-bear, is a tree-living marsupial. It can only survive in certain eastern parts of Australia, the area where the eucalyptus tree it feeds on grows. To live elsewhere, such as in a zoo, it would need an assured supply of eucalyptus leaves.

CATS ARE SAID to have nine lives because they can fall from a height and survive: the theory is that, like a self-righting 'unsinkable' lifeboat, they turn over in the air and always end the right way up, on their feet. In fact, cats are not proof against injury, and if they fall awkwardly can easily hurt themselves. So never drop a cat out of a window, even from a modest height, for it may be one of the unlucky ones without nine lives.

One cat, however, who might claim to have had its share of extra lifespan, survived a fall from the eleventh floor of a London block of flats in 1965. It slipped on its owner's balcony and dropped 36m, which means that it was probably travelling at around 112km/h when it hit the ground. It was not only uninjured but fit enough to walk away.

THE REVEREND GEOFFREY HOWARD of Salford, near Manchester, England, set out early in 1975 on what must surely be one of the oddest journeys in a decade that has seen some very odd journeys indeed. His objective: to push a wheelbarrow across the Sahara Desert. It was no ordinary garden wheelbarrow, but a special one designed by the Engineering Department of an Oxford University College. Fitted with a sail, it was inspired by a Chinese model.

Soon after brief training sessions on the beach of a nearby seaside resort, the perambulating parson started his hazardous journey at Beni-Abbes, Algeria, in the north-west corner of the Sahara. He planned to cover the 3,200 *km* to Kano, Nigeria, on the other side of the desert in a hundred days.

By early February he had reached the half-way mark, but not without mishap. He was nearly burned to death when his tent caught fire and some essential supplies were destroyed. He also had trouble with the wheel of his barrow and had to do some makeshift repairs. An escort of two soldiers and a Land Rover was accompanying him but he refused to hitch a lift in the vehicle even after his troubles.

In spite of these mishaps he completed his wheelbarrow walk six days ahead of the scheduled one hundred, having maintained the astonishing daily average of over 32*km*. Yet he himself lost only a couple of kilos on the journey.

Why did he do it? Primarily to raise funds for charity, but also, as he put it, 'because it had never been done before'.

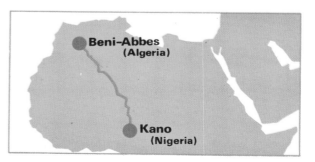

Beni-Abbes
(Algeria)

Kano
(Nigeria)

STRANGEST escape from death

HE WAS A TWENTY-YEAR-OLD SERVANT called John Lee. In January 1885 at Exeter in the west of England, Lee was condemned to death for killing his employer, although the evidence was circumstantial and did not convincingly establish his guilt.

During his agonizing three weeks awaiting execution, his mother had a dream — indeed, as it turned out, a premonition. In her dream she saw the noose and the scaffold clearly, watched the hangman pull the lever and then saw her son still standing, apparently unscathed, on the scaffold. She recounted this dream to the prison warders who officially recorded and signed the statement.

At the hour appointed for the execution the chief hangman stood with his hand on the lever that would operate the 'drop'. When he pulled the lever, the trap-door beneath the condemned man would drop away suddenly, and the body would swing downwards into the space beneath the trap-door. That is how it had always happened and that is what Berry the hangman expected to happen on that historic morning. Opposite Berry, standing on

the trap-door with a bag over his head, noose around his neck, arms and legs pinioned, stood John Lee calmly awaiting his end.

'Have you anything to say?' Berry asked the prisoner. 'Drop away', whispered Lee hoarsely. The hangman's hand jerked, the lever clanged and — nothing happened. The trap-door stayed firmly closed with Lee standing on it very much alive. The astonished Berry could hardly believe his eyes. Never in the long history of the 'drop' system had there been a single mechanical failure. He pulled a second time. The lever moved but not the trapdoor; it remained obstinately shut. By now as bewildered as Lee, the exasperated Berry tried a third time. Again the trap-door refused to open. 'Take him away', said the hangman. When the story of John Lee's escape was known, the public reaction was mixed. Some said it was an act of God: an innocent man had been saved; it was a miracle, a sign. The authorities were also impressed, for they commuted Lee's sentence to life imprisonment.

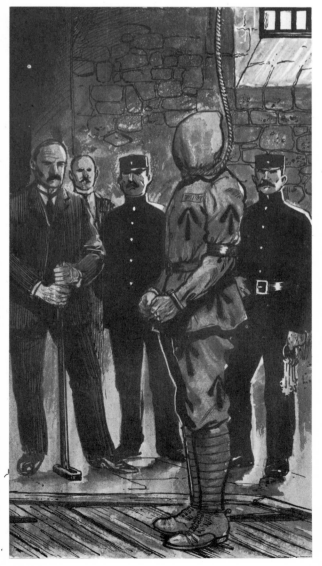

In the years that followed a lot of words were written, a film made and a ballad composed about the man they couldn't hang. Lee became a folk hero to some while he languished in prison. Various theories were put forward about the 'miracle' and why the trap-door had failed to operate. It was said that overnight rain had affected the mechanism and caused the failure. It was said that a friendly warder had wedged it to prevent its opening. The mystery deepened fifty years after the event when a journalist on a local paper in Devon published a long article claiming that Lee had been innocent and the murderer was, in fact, a well-known local celebrity whom he could not identify for various reasons. No explanation ever did come to light. John Lee served twenty-two years in jail before he was released. He married, moved to London and lived rather an obscure life, doubtless unable to forget that he had become a legend, a freak of criminal history, as 'the man they couldn't hang'. It is believed that he died in the U.S.A. in 1933.

STRANGEST power...olympics

THE ODDEST SPORTING OLYMPIAD is undoubtedly the Eskimo Olympics, held annually in Alaska. Nothing quite as normal or dull as sprinting, jumping and throwing will satisfy these enthusiastic Eskimos. They go in for such contests as ear-pulling, fish-cutting, seal-skinning, blubber-eating, knuckle-hopping and blanket-tossing, not to mention ear-weighting. The winners of some of these events lifted 8*kg* of lead weights by the ears, ate a large steak of raw blubber (whale meat) in 15 seconds, skinned a 1·8*m*-long, 112*kg* seal in one minute flat, and hit the ceiling after a 12*m* blanket toss.

'DOWSING' USED TO BE called water-divining. A dowser is a person who has the peculiar gift of being able to detect water deep in the ground by using a simple pendulum or forked rod. One present-day dowsing family, a father and four sons in Yorkshire, England, uses pieces of bent wire which turn inwards when water is detected. The pendulum, a wooden ball hung on a thread, swings madly when the holder passes over water. The forked rod, usually two pieces of wood or whalebone joined to form a V-shape, is held by the dowser in his clenched fists. When there is a reaction the rod twitches violently and is tugged earthwards as though by some mighty magnetic force.

Dowsers have found water where geologists, with all their scientific equipment and knowledge, have failed. Some can exercise the gift a great distance away from the site, like the parson who detected water on a tea plantation in Uganda by using his dowsing powers on maps of the area, thousands of miles away. The spot on the map indicated by the dowser proved to be the site of water. Not only water can be discovered. Using their simple, crude equipment dowsers have detected oil, minerals, and even buried treasure. Some map dowsers specialize in tracing lost persons and have assisted police investigations by indicating the whereabouts of the missing persons. How is it done? What mystical power does the dowser have that enables him to trace the invisible and sometimes far-distant object? The answer must remain a mystery.

THE AVERAGE COW has 36m of small intestine.

DOLPHINS SLEEP for only two hours or so at a time and always with one eye closed.

A WELL-KNOWN CHEMICAL COMPANY in England reduced by 75 per cent complaints about the objectionable smell of fumes from their chimneys by setting up a nose patrol. The sniffers had to pass tests to prove they had at least 90 per cent accuracy in detecting smells and then make regular patrols to identify and report on them. Every complaint, not necessarily about smells from their factory, was investigated.

THE MATING CALL of the male toci-toci beetle is tapping on a stone. The vibrations made are undetectable by the most sensitive microphone but can be picked up by a female toci-toci 5km away.

A SNAKE at London Zoo has been fitted with a glass eye.

THE U.S.A. COAST GUARD research centre has found a way of identifying tankers which pollute their coastline by discharging oil illegally offshore. Apparently a ship leaves an unmistakable chemical 'fingerprint' on the oil carried in its hold, which shows up on any discharge, so it is possible to take a sample of the oil slick in the sea and match it to the offending tanker. It's a slow job: no less than 250 ships were tested before one recent identification was made.

EVERY YEAR, IN BRITAIN ALONE, a quarter of a million frogs are used for research. Thousands are killed on the roads or die when their traditional breeding grounds in the countryside are destroyed by development schemes, motorways and the like. Pesticides, farm mechanization and the pollution or complete destruction of ponds and ditches have also taken their severe toll of this harmless, timid and likeable little amphibian. When you consider that out of every thousand tadpoles hatched only about ten survive to become young frogs and that a child may innocently destroy in a moment spawn containing a quarter of a million eggs, you can see why the common frog's existence is threatened by modern society. Indeed the frog, turned out of its natural habitat, is taking to the garden pond. Its future survival may well depend on that small pool at the bottom of the domestic garden. One man who has done more than anyone to conserve the common-or-garden frog is Ernest Ibbetson of St Albans, an historic town twenty miles from London. He has made a serious study of the frog for some thirty years and every springtime he has about seven hundred frogs in his garden. But it's not Mr Ibbetson's lifelong devotion to the frog nor the size of his garden population that is so surprising. It is the fact that he has bred an *orange* frog, believed to be unique in the world.

This brand-new breed, a brilliant, translucent orange, occurred by mutation during the course of the colony's breeding season. Mr Ibbetson refuses to sell any of his beautiful orange frogs, even if one could put a price on them, and they live under the strictest security to safeguard them from vandals.

STRANGEST ship...city

BUILT IN THE 1850s by The Jointed Ship Company of London, the *Connector* must be one of the strangest ships ever made. She was constructed in three hinged sections, supposedly to 'ride' the waves safely and smoothly in high seas. The sections could be separated for fast unloading of her cargo — thought to have been coal.

THE GREEK PHILOSOPHER PLATO is our authority for the legend of the lost city of Atlantis, the beautiful, wealthy and contented island in the Atlantic Ocean off the Straits of Gibraltar. According to the legend, it was governed by the sea-god Poseidon (Neptune) until a series of earthquakes caused Atlantis to sink into the ocean. The Lost City of Atlantis has intrigued scholars for centuries. In mediaeval times many people believed it had existed although there was no evidence to prove this common belief. Then, in 1967, a Minoan city was unearthed on a Greek island in the Aegean. This city had been buried by volcanic ash in 1500 BC and some archaeologists

still think it might once have been part of Atlantis.

Was there such a place and if so, where was it? America, Scandinavia, the Canary Islands and even Palestine have all been suggested as other likely locations for the mysterious city. True or false, legend or fact, the idea of a buried city under the ocean inspired two famous novelists, Conan Doyle and Jules Verne, to write what could be called early science-fiction stories. Verne's *20,000 Leagues Under the Sea* also inspired a Walt Disney film. A scene from it appears below. (*The Maracot Deep* was the title of the book by Doyle, better known for creating the famous detective Sherlock Holmes.)

Index

Conversion table

Length

1 millimetre (*m*) =   0·0394 inches
1 centimetre (*cm*) =   0·3937 inches
1 metre (*m*)   = 39·3701 inches
1 kilometre (*km*) =   0·6214 miles

Area

1 square centimetre =   0·155 square inches
1 square metre   = 1550 square inches
1 square kilometre =   247·105 acres
1 hectare   =   2·471 acres

Volume

1 litre (*l*) = 1000 cubic metres
            =   0·2199 gallons (or 1·7597 pints)
            =   3·5315 cubic feet

Weight

1 milligram (*mg*)   = 0·000036 ounces
1 gram (*g*)   = 0·0362 ounces
1 kilogram (*kg*)   = 2·2046 pounds
1 tonne (1000*kg*) = 0·9842 tons